POSSIBILITIES UNLIMITED

STORIES TO INSPIRE YOU TO ACHIEVE THE IMPOSSIBLE

PRESENTED BY

LES BROWN *AND*
DR. CHERYL WOOD

To Ann,
Thank you for being an amazing person! Remember - With God, life truly is unlimited!!

Anita

Publication Layout & Design: Literary Bae
www.literarybae.com

CONTENTS

FOREWORD

By Les Brown

You have something special, you have GREATNESS in YOU!

If you have followed my career or heard me speak, then you know that I believe that all of us were born with a purpose and that we all have great gifts inside just waiting to be unleashed and shared with the world.

As much as I know this to be true, I can't tell you how many people I've met or who send me messages asking me to help them tap into or discover their purpose and the impact they're meant to make.

These people are a lot like I was many years ago, they are suffering from what I call, Possibility Blindness. They can't see the possibilities, potential, and promise that life holds for them. I understand how that feels. They feel like it's possible for others, but feel that they either aren't worthy or don't have what it takes to impact lives, walk into their purpose, and create a legacy.

Have you ever felt this way? I did for quite a long time, until I finally discovered that there are limitless possibilities connected to my very being!

Guess what? You have limitless possibilities connected to your very being too!

I am excited to share with you Dr. Cheryl Wood's latest groundbreaking book, POSSIBILITIES UNLIMITED.

We all need a little coaching from time to time to help us walk into and/or remain focused on the global impact we're meant to make in the world with our unique gifts and I'm glad that Cheryl is here to provide us with this gem. Prepare to uncover and overcome the mental and emotional barriers in your life that are blocking you from pursuing all of your possibilities and experiencing the fulfillment you can receive by sharing your gifts.

Dr. Wood shares with us that no matter what seems to be broken, imperfect, or flawed in you, that you can still have greatness in you and you can create great impact with your unique DNA. Now is the time for you to explore and unleash the possibilities inside of you!

There is no one in this world quite like you and we need what you have to offer.

I hope you're ready to transform your mind and your life, because reading these pages will certainly push you forward and accelerate your journey into greatness, purpose and impact.

I keep this book close by me to feel inspired and motivated. I'm sure you will too!

Remember, you have a unique fingerprint that no one can duplicate and no one can create the impact that can only be felt when you boldly execute the limitless possibilities that are inside of you!

That's my story and I'm sticking to it.

Les Brown
Speaker, Author, Trainer

INTRODUCTION

By Dr. Cheryl Wood

Compilation Visionary of Possibilities Unlimited
17x Best-Selling Author | International Empowerment Speaker |
2x TEDx Speaker | Master Speaker Development
Coach | Leadership Expert

Your possibilities are unlimited! You are just getting started! Your best is still in front of you! I need you to know that you are an irreplaceable expression of life, a one-of-a-kind precious masterpiece, the likes of which no one will ever see again. You are powerful beyond all measure. And you have everything you need to achieve the things that seem impossible in your life. In fact, turning what appears impossible into the possible is in your DNA. You were born from greatness to manifest greatness! But, in order to manifest everything connected to your greatness and your limitless possibilities, you must first believe that you are capable of accomplishing anything you set your mind to. You must develop a mindset of determination and a spirit of tenacity to press through anything that hinders you from becoming the greatest version of yourself.

From this moment forward, even in the face of all your fears, doubts and self-limiting beliefs, I challenge you to boldly embrace that you are uniquely designed and have a divine calling on your life that is bigger than you! The calling on your life is about the countless people who will be impacted and inspired to pursue their possibilities because you developed the courage to pursue what seemed impossible in your own life.

In this book, you will be reminded that becoming the best version of yourself will require ongoing courage, tenacity, drive, ambition, determination and commitment. On your journey to fulfilling unlimited possibilities, you will face challenges, obstacles, roadblocks and setbacks, but your internal strength will equip you to bounce back from anything standing in the way of your destiny. In the words of Nelson Mandela, "It always seems impossible until it's done." You have what it takes to soar beyond all limitations. Don't forget to remind yourself, on a daily basis, who you are, 'whose you are,' and what you are capable of.

As you immerse yourself in the stories and messages contained in this book, it is my hope that your internal desire to win big, play full out, and raise the bar on your own expectations of what's possible in your life will be ignited. I challenge you to reinforce for yourself, that in spite of your past and all the struggles you've been through, you broke through, pressed through and kept getting back up. Regardless of who counted you out, you proved them wrong, and that means you were born for a time such as this to keep striving, growing, elevating and accomplishing what seems impossible.

In my own life, I had to go on a personal journey of discovering I was enough, regardless of my past. As a young girl who was raised in scarcity in an inner-city housing project in Baltimore, Maryland, I assumed my life would be dictated by my environment. I assumed people would judge who I could become based on where I had come from, and that I would be another statistic like many of the other youth in my neighborhood. But there was a turning point when I started to shift my mindset and my perspective, deciding that I didn't want to be a statistic. I wanted to rise above my past, achieve the impossible, and become a change agent in the world who would impact women's lives globally! Once I made the decision, I allowed my actions to come into alignment with my decision.

As I have continued to acknowledge that I'm enough just as I am, it has positioned me to become more confident, driven and determined in sharing my voice, using my gifts and making my mark in the world instead of simply staying quiet and accepting whatever life hands me. I have become a willing vessel to empower, educate and equip women globally with the tools to pursue their own possibilities, develop new levels of confidence in who they have the potential to become, and boldly come to the front of the room to share their voice and their gifts.

As you take a deep dive into the stories shared in *Possibilities Unlimited*, it is my hope that you feel enlightened, reenergized and reignited for the impact and legacy you are meant to create in the world through your own possibilities. It is my deep hope that you'll be reminded of your own strength and that you'll dream a little bigger, fight a little harder for what you want, bounce back a little quicker when you get knocked down, and never ever give up. You were not created to be ordinary; you were designed to be EXTRAordinary!

I celebrate each of the co-authors of the *Possibilities Unlimited* book project for selflessly sharing their stories and testimonies of soaring beyond the impossible. Each story will propel you to develop a new mindset, new attitude, new behaviors and new patterns in order to live your best life. As you immerse yourself into the *Possibilities Unlimited* book, remember that you matter and the world needs you too!

Dr. Cheryl Wood
Compilation Visionary of *Possibilities Unlimited*
WEBSITE: www.cherylempowers.com
EMAIL: info@cherylwoodempowers.com
SOCIAL MEDIA: @CherylEmpowers

PURPOSE ISN'T ALWAYS PRETTY

By Niadu O. Allen

As I am sitting here refusing to allow my mind to be broken by grief, it is from a wealthy place in Christ that I share my endurance in pain yet continuing in purpose. My only daughter, at the age of 29, was murdered on June 18, 2021, by her children's father who subsequently also killed himself! With me now taking care of my four grandchildren, which was never a part of my vision board, you would think my destiny would just say, *girl stop, it's too painful, and you're too weak and distraught to try and go on any longer. How dare you keep going against the pressures of life? Girl, just give up and die to your dreams, goals, achievements and love. Just let it go and simply exist.*

Yet, there is something inside of me that God has placed that won't let me give up. Her name is Purpose. Purpose has been thriving on the fragments of life support refusing to let go. Purpose kept me when my mom died at 29 years old, when my sister was murdered at 29, when I suffered a miscarriage at 29 and now my daughter being murdered at 29. Yet, God's purposeful hands won't let go of this purposed woman.

I found myself, as so many other people do, asking God what is my purpose in life? Based on statistics, I'm not supposed to be successful. I'm not supposed to keep getting up and trying again. When I tried to open a transitional home, I received so many no's any normal person would just give up. But here I am once again, refusing to drink the Kool-Aid that has been presented to me, refusing to accept that this is just how life must be, and once again, fighting for those who don't have a voice. Fighting to change systemic laws that keep families in a cycle of poverty. Fighting to bring awareness to a system that has rules everyone didn't agree upon. Fighting to help women and children rise above the limitations society has placed on them. I am here as evidence that you too can rise and live above grief, pain, disappointments, and failures.

I've realized in life that sometimes purpose is painful. So many times, we try to dress up purpose and present it perfect and beautiful without any scars, marks, blemishes, or flaws. But, we aren't being honest with ourselves and with others regarding the realities of life. Though it may appear that our purpose is flourishing on top, underneath the surface we're drowning in a sea of hardships. The reality is that most of our purpose has been birthed from loss and painful experiences. Whether it's the loss of a job, a business deal, the death of a loved one, divorce, or the deceitfulness of friends, we can all relate to disappointments in life. But if we really look at the blueprints of life, we can see purpose has been strategically crafted in.

I encourage anyone who may have experienced blow after blow and hit after hit and your life has not gone as planned, to still believe that you have great purpose in you. I know now that defeat and fear can keep you down and shackled and try to ride along on your journey. But you have to tell them that their fare has run out! No more free rides in my mind and I am not your personal Uber. When you get to a place in your life when you can say, "I have nothing to lose" it's the perfect time to get out of the boat of safety and swim. When you have lost everything, you're not worried about your family and friends advising you to live normal. You realize that you have suffered for the greatness that is on the inside of you and it is your time to conquer it all.

Now you can either choose to sit your purpose-full self in fear and defeat OR you could choose purpose as your portion and see the many possible opportunities that are presented even though they may come wrapped up in struggles and challenges.

Fear and defeat have more than one way of robbing us of our purpose in life. They also strip us of our time, talents, gifts, love for self and others, and our identity. But, do you realize that you are the key to someone else's lock? Others may be praying and seeking God for clarity and direction, while all along you are the master key to not only helping but solving so many of their problems. And I know one question that may be in your mind: What about me? As you open the doors for others, there will be revolving doors opening for you. I'm a firm believer that what you help to make happen for someone else, there is a community of supporters that will make it happen for you.

Have you ever eaten something that tasted good but the dish wasn't pleasing to the eyes? I tried Indian food for the first time a few years ago. It was curry chicken pasta which had so many yellow foreign vegetables surrounding it that the chicken was almost unrecognizable. After one bite, I asked, "What is in this?" It was the tablespoons of curry that had awakened the other ingredients and brought it all together. That was the purpose of the curry. Maybe YOU are that last missing tablespoon in the recipe of life that will create a legacy full of richness and power!

BIO

Niadu O Allen has been in healthcare management for more than 25 years. She has mentored women, both professionally and personally, to continue in life's purpose. She has taught life skills classes for women as they are re-entering society. She has received a Women's Phenomenal Award for her work, along with other awards for her work in the community and continuing efforts to bring awareness to laws that divide families. Niadu is seeking to open a transitional home for women and children in honor of her daughter, Johnesia and her sister, Anonda.

Follow Naidu on social media at:

Facebook: Niadu Deliberately Chosen Allen

Instagram: niadu_o

KICKING DOUBT IN THE FACE WITH MY CONVERSES ON

By Sandra M. Braxton, PMP, MBA

I was exhausted. Not physically but mentally. So much so that I landed in the emergency room. I'd never felt such pain in my chest before and was sure I was having a heart attack. I was afraid because I've heard that you can't ignore things like this. Some women have died because they thought it was just a pain that they can walk off or take a pain pill to feel better in the morning. I wasn't going out like that. I logged off my laptop and immediately called my husband at his job to tell him that I was going to the ER and to meet me there. My husband arrived and they brought him back to my room. I've never seen him so concerned. He knows that I don't like to go to the hospital so if I suggested it, I must have really been in pain. After the nurses retrieved the readings from the machine I was hooked to, the doctor entered the room. He was very calm and nice which put me at ease. I must not have been dying otherwise they'd have been rushing me out of the room. The doctor asked me again about my symptoms. I told him that I was having chest pains and I felt as if I couldn't catch my breath. What he said next would stick with me forever. He said "Whatever stress you have in your life you've got to get rid of it before it gets rid of you. You're not having a heart attack but you just experienced a panic attack and it's warning you to make changes."

This physical experience was a direct result of what was going on inside my head. I was overwhelmed, miserable and felt like there was no way out. I couldn't breathe because I felt trapped. From that day forward, I made the decision to choose me over everything.

I began my career as a network technician and shortly thereafter got promoted into management as a Project Manager. After obtaining my PM Certification, I was able to command six-figure salaries. For the most part, I enjoyed what I did but I got used to the lifestyle that my salary afforded us. International travel, world class food and shopping...especially the shopping. I love me some shoes -- got a pair for each outfit. And Converses are so darn versatile. You can dress them up or down but you're always fly with a pair on.

So, when did it all change? Most of us had been subjected to a company downsize. At one point, I was part of a four-person management team responsible for eight consultants. In a matter of hours that changed to a one-person management team of just me. My workload doubled and in turn my stress level intensified. I went from singing in the car on my way to the office to dragging myself out of bed and mustering up the energy to get dressed. I thought, *there must be a better way and I've got to figure it out for goodness sake.*

The entire time I worked my corporate position I had a business on the side. I've always had that entrepreneurial spirit. Most of my businesses began as hobbies and didn't make lots of money but taught me how to run a business, how to deal with clients and that I had control over what my businesses became. My business's growth usually matched the amount of time I put into them. My travel agency, The Braxton Agency, was different from all the others. I've had a passion for traveling since taking my first plane ride on my way to Air Force Basic Training. The feeling I get from helping people plan trips to places that they've only dreamt about is indescribable. Let's be real though, passion doesn't pay the bills. I was afraid to take the leap of faith to focus solely on my business, but even more fearful of what I would become if I didn't. After much contemplation and prayer, I wrote out my resignation letter and didn't look back. I bet all my chips on myself and my business.

Riding home after turning in my badge, my files and my laptop, I found myself singing again. It had been four months since that ER visit and I felt like the weight of the world had been lifted from my shoulders.

So, I ask you, have you lost your song, sis? If so, then you must get it back. Oftentimes we lose ourselves in the pursuit of happiness. But we must examine what truly brings us joy. One thing I know is that God will never take us anywhere without giving us the tools to survive. There is light at the end of every tunnel. Put on your Converses and get to kicking.

How did I do it?

During those four months I devised a plan of how I would pay down debt and be able to survive in the lean time that was forthcoming.

1. I ceased shopping.
2. I paid off my car and as many credit cards as I could.
3. We postponed a few trips that we had scheduled.

I am grateful to my husband for supporting my decision although he couldn't see the full vision at the time. I won't lie to you. The sacrifices we made were painful, but not as painful as staying in the stressful situation that my corporate position presented. No amount of money is worth that.

BIO

I reside in a suburb of Atlanta with my husband Octavian and our 2 doggies; Kali Marie & Zoe Brooklyn. Originally from Rocky Mount, NC, I proudly served in the U.S. Air Force and am a War Veteran. I am also a member of Zeta Phi Beta Sorority Incorporated. For the past two years, I have been solely working at The Braxton Agency curating travel adventures.

My husband and I co-authored a Book entitled "Why Not Us" available on Amazon and Kindle. Many others suffer from infertility in silence. We share our story so that it may help another couple not feel alone in their journey.

I am currently working towards obtaining my real estate license in the state of Georgia and look forward to being able to assist clients reach the goal of home ownership.

Website: www.thebraxtonagency.com

Follow me on social media at @TheBraxtonAgency and @AuthorSandraMBraxton

RESTORING THE HEALER

By Nikki Bullock

During the Bowie State University 2013 commencement, while keynote speaker, First Lady Michelle Obama was addressing my class, I found myself reflecting on several events that led to this moment. During one of the most challenging seasons of my life, I discovered the ability to conquer the impossible. Restoration of life balance is an essential principle that influences our ability to reach our full life potential. We are inherently designed to defy life's obstacles, while seeking the boundless possibilities that are embedded within our purpose. I discovered my passion for the mental health and wellness field while serving in the US Army. I determined that higher education would supply me with the essential tools to achieve my career goals.

Ten years ago, while pursuing my degree I suffered a mild stroke. I thought it would be impossible to accomplish the goal of completing a master's degree in Counseling Psychology.

It was during the midst of this adversity, that I was introduced to my unlimited possibilities.

It was my typical Tuesday summer morning drive into work. I would transport my son to daycare and head to work. While approaching a traffic stop, a tingling sensation began to intensify in my right arm and hand. Initially, I thought my extremity was falling asleep; however, the tingling sensation evolved into a numbing feeling. My right hand began sliding down the steering wheel. I instinctively grabbed the steering wheel with my other hand to regain control of the car. As I struggled to regain feeling in my hand and arm, I started moving my shoulders back and forth. When I only felt numbness, it created an unsettling anxiety. I quickly realized that something else was occurring to my body. I determined at this time that I must seek immediate medical attention.

We were within a few blocks from my son's daycare provider and he did not appear to notice anything. I summoned my strength and pulled into the parking lot dropping him off. Navigating through the daycare, my panic increased as I struggled to carry my son to his classroom. As I kissed my son goodbye, my mind was racing and wondering why no one seemed to notice my condition. While returning to my vehicle my thoughts immediately transitioned to obtaining medical attention.

After spending several hours in the ER undergoing a series of tests, the doctor informed me that I suffered a mild stroke. My mind began to race! I thought to myself, how could this even be possible! I was a 33-year-old healthy woman with no pre-existing medical conditions. After the doctor left the room, I went to the bathroom and stared into the mirror. Immediately I noticed a slight paralysis to the right side of my face. In that moment I felt an unsettling sense of defeat radiating beneath my bones. There was so much at stake in this moment. I can recall thinking to myself "I don't have time to get sick. How much damage has occurred? Would I recover?"

There I sat in the ER, a single mom, mental health professional, and a full-time graduate student. In this moment I felt powerless, fearful, and wondered if I would ever attain my goals. I never imagined that a mild stroke would be the catalyst to my own self-healing.

During Recovery it became apparent that I would have to reevaluate the path that led me into this moment. I was oblivious of the fact that, while I was striving to achieve greater access to heal and help others, I failed to recognize my own need for self-care. While traveling this road, it became apparent that self-care was the vital component of healing myself. I adopted a consistent self-care regimen that included: adequate rest, improved nutrition, and increased exercise. Self-care must include consistent restoration to ensure the exterior and interior parts of self are in alignment.

Just as the road to recovery revealed the previous principles for healing, I discovered that establishing personal boundaries are equally important. One of the greatest gifts I gave myself was the ability to say "No". Utilizing personal boundaries allows you to protect the power of your purpose. The assignment you have been purposed with may remain the same, however, the strategy to accomplish the mission may require adjustments.

Following months of self-care, constant self-reflection, and prayer, I felt restored. It was at that moment I realized that I conquered my impossible. It is through our quest to seek our dreams and aspirations, that we discover our capacity to reach our unlimited possibilities.

Five Self-Help Tips to Restore the Healer:

1) **Embrace** practicing consistent selfcare. Be kind to yourself. **"Even heroes have a place to hang their capes."** Incorporate a daily self-care regimen.

2) **Acknowledge** that you require personal and professional boundaries. Set your boundaries and stick to them. Embrace your "No's".

3) **Timing** - Be realistic about what you can accomplish. Prioritize your time with intention.

4) **Reevaluate**- Set a daily schedule to evaluate your day and acknowledge and consider the things you did well.

5) **Reflection**-Think about the things you would like to do better. Self-reflection is the key to self-awareness. It allows us to look impartially at our ideas, feelings, emotions, and actions. Through this practice, we can allow ourselves grace.

BIO

Nikki Bullock began her career with exemplary service in the United States Army. She has dedicated over 20 years providing mental health services for at-risk populations, in New York City and Washington D.C. Metro areas. Nikki leveraged her experience in the mental health field towards an extensive career in social and psychological counseling. She holds a BA in Sociology, MA in Counseling Psychology, and is the CEO and founder of Restore Wellness & Consulting Services, LLC. Nikki specializes in trauma care and is a Certified Life Mapping Coach based in Maryland. Her holistic approach brings clarity, direction, and positive support for her clients. By identifying where growth is desired, setting goals and objectives, and accountability, clients will reach their highest goals and dreams. Connect with me at: @nikki_bullockrestorewellness

THIRTEEN YEARS A SLAVE FOR MY DREAMS

By Dr. Elizabeth A. Carter

It was March 2019 in Orlando, Florida. We were in line alphabetically. My goal was to walk across the stage without:

- falling because of the high heels I shouldn't have worn
- fainting from overheating in my hot velvet gown, or
- crying and having my face look like a sad clown in my photos.

It was commencement day, the ceremonial hooding where I proudly walked across the stage and heard my new, official name, "**DOCTOR** Elizabeth A. Carter."

While I waited, my journey replayed in my head, which had begun 13 years prior.

Fears, False Information, and Facts

In 2006, I received my second master's degree from the same university where I stood to hear my new official name. I envisioned the possibility of me one day being like the parade of Ph.D. candidates I saw with excited faces. They knew they had created their legacies. But I had lots of apprehensions. Memories of student loan payments haunted me. I was not interested in repeating those experiences. Another thought was, *"Will I get the return on the investment?"* I knew what I could do with a Ph.D. in Education, but I was already having trouble navigating the 'traditional' finance career ladder with a second master's degree outside of the finance discipline.

Also, at that time, the internet only highlighted the top one percent world changers and the bottom twenty percent failures. That information shaped my perception as I was never in the top one percent of anything and failure was a curse word in my household. I held Ph.Ds in high regard. I imagined people who'd earned them as brilliant thinkers whose research changed the trajectory of the world. I had no life changing ideas. Plus, I knew very smart people who started the Ph.D. process, quit before completion, and now lived with a lesser accomplishment, the "ABD" (All but Dissertation), which confirmed my concerns that success is highly unlikely.

My myths were dismissed in May 2011 after a conversation with a family friend. Energized and anxious after the encouragement I received, I enrolled the following semester. Because it was a last-minute decision, I took out a loan for the first year and set a budget to save for the subsequent years and pay off the loan.

Failure and Frustration Along the Way

As an alum of the master's program, some requirements in the Ph.D. program were waived. In my mind, that was a way to cut down on the financial burden of the program and the time required to complete it. Little did I know, a series of events would result in me reaching the maximum time allotted for completion of the program and facing possible dismissal without the degree.

- The major project before the dissertation phase is the Doctoral Comprehensive Examination (AKA 'Comps'). Underestimation, perfectionism, and poor time management resulted in me submitting an incomplete exam and receiving a "no pass" grade. The penalty was two quarters of writing courses to re-qualify for the exam.

- Once I passed Comps on the second try, the next hurdle was choosing a dissertation topic and finding a group that would permit me to use their members as "the sample." My dissertation committee rejected every idea I suggested:

    ◦ First topic- My committee did not feel it was robust enough for a study.
    ◦ Second topic- My committee felt the sample size would be too small to provide anonymity for my group.
    ◦ First organization I selected for my sample- I had first-line leader approval, but upper leadership was not interested in the study.
    ◦ Second organization I selected- It received approval, but it took a year to have it finalized.

- There were moments the system was against me. I started questioning my intelligence, intention, and interest in finishing. I was close to joining my 'ABD' friends, and self-doubt was rising.

- I was laid off from my job in June 2016, which provided me the ability to focus full-time on the dissertation, but along with the job search, the motivation to write was a daily challenge.

Finding the Finish Line

Despite all I went through, I did not quit. With the strength that came from friends' and family's encouragement, I progressed to my dissertation defense call, the last step to graduate. It was October 14, 2018. Hearing the words "approved with a few edits" was humbling, relieving, and exciting.

Back to Orlando

Smiling to myself and silently thanking those who assisted me in the journey, I beamed as the procession started moving. I handed my doctoral hood to the dean, and she placed it over my head while another said, "Presenting Doctor Elizabeth A. Carter." I smiled for the camera and heard my mother yell from the audience, "That's my baby!" I shook the graduate panel's hands and exited the stage. I did not fall, faint, or cry.

Forever Grateful

Since 2019, my research has been referenced in presentations, books, and articles. I still work in finance and use my Ph.D. skills on the job. I am called Dr. Carter by many out of respect, and they have no idea how much those words mean to me.

So many people are afraid to start, they quit after one obstacle, or they let the rumors and haters get inside their heads and take over. Use me as a testimonial: The possibilities are unlimited! I was a 'B' student in high school and worse in undergrad. If you had asked me 20 years ago where I would be today, 'Dr. Carter' would not have been my answer. Knowledge can come from education, experience, or exposure, and when you fall, knowledge will always get you back on your feet.

No matter the dream or aspiration, the process is similar. We are working and waiting for the reward. When we hear the word *slave*, naturally, we think of its basic definition--being controlled by some-one else. I use a different definition, though. *Slave* is *working excessively hard*. That is what we must do to get what we want. When you do feel like a slave, keep the following in mind.

> S – Separate the facts, fallacies, and fears. These could keep you stuck.

L - Listen to the fans in your life. They will keep you energized.

A - Acknowledge that there will be sacrifices. Plan for the worse and hope for the best.

V – Visualize the future. Stay true to your WHY.

E - Enjoy the journey. That is where the growth and transformation occurs.

I was a slave to my dreams, and every day I am blessed and thankful for the outcome.

BIO

Dr. Elizabeth A. Carter is a finance leader, speaker, career coach, and best-selling author. With over 25 years working in corporate settings, Dr. Carter's unique combination of financial acumen and knowledge empowerment has provided her the opportunity to lead, mentor and develop others. Dr. Carter is especially enthusiastic about working to "Break the Eight", as records show that only eight percent of the country's African American population have jobs in management or better.

Her company AAPPEAL empowers women of color in STEM industries to master their mindset, money dependencies, and their mouths (just keepin' it real) which are holding them back in their companies. Through her books, frameworks, coaching programs, and keynote presentations, women gain clarity, confidence, and control of their careers. They 'Level-up' their purpose and presence which can propel their career progression up, across, or even out, if necessary!

Website: https://www.eac-aappeal.com

Facebook, Twitter, Instagram - eacaappeal

DON'T JUST DREAM IT...LIVE IT!

By Arnita R. Craighead

Have you ever had a dream so close that you can taste it, smell it, even reach out and touch it?

What did you do with that dream? Did you work to fulfill it? Water it, nurture it and watch it grow?

Or did you give up on it? Did you allow it to just be a dream and drift away? If you didn't fulfill it – why? And better yet, what's stopping you now?

Let me share something with you: the only thing stopping you – is YOU. And here's the question you have to ask yourself – *why are you holding you back*?

You may be saying, *it's too late.*

It's been so long.

I had that dream when I was five years old and now, I'm 35.

I've been through so much and there is no way my dreams can come true now.

We've all gone through something. Heartbreak. Loss. Layoffs. Being fired. Repossession. Eviction. Foreclosure. Nervous breakdowns. Any of these can have devastating outcomes. However, you don't have to let that define you. What matters is how you deal with the hand you've been dealt. If you choose to be a victim, then you will never move forward. You will continually make excuses that keep you stuck in your present circumstances. But, if you choose to be a victor, then you will learn from your experiences and move forward. From there, you can live a life of endless possibilities, bigger than you ever imagined.

The way to live that life of endless possibilities is by tapping into yourself. God gave us all gifts and talents to utilize and share with the world. Why are you keeping yours under wraps? You're hiding what someone else needs! That benefits no one, not even you. You have to start somewhere and the easiest way to do it is to take the first step. How do you do that? Put one foot right in front of the other. Is it scary? Absolutely! But what's scarier, staying stuck where you are or pressing forward to see what life has in store? Take a chance! Start that business. Apply for that job. Go out on that date. Write that book. Have that family. Build that house. Invest that money. Audition for that movie. Take that vacation. DO IT ALL!!

I want to leave you with something to think about. I previously watched a movie called *Heart and Souls*. It was a cute little movie in which four people died, and after their deaths, they had one last chance to resolve their lives. They had to accomplish this through a little boy they befriended after they first died. One of the four, a gentleman, had wanted to sing professionally but when given opportunities to sing, he always got terrible stage fright and could never go through with it. He would always start sweating, his hands would get clammy, and his knees would knock so badly he wouldn't even be able to stand up straight! In the movie, he was given one last chance to finally live out his dream through the little boy who was a grown man at the time. And you know what? All the deceased man continued to say was, *"I'm going to fail. I can't do it. I'm a big failure."*

The young man looked at him and said, *"No offense. But you were a failure because you never tried."*

Let me ask YOU a question...would you want someone to say that about you?

Would you want to say that about yourself?

Don't you want to at least try?

They say the richest place in the world is the graveyard. Why? Because unfortunately, so many people never try and they die with their dreams still locked inside. Unlike the scenario above, this is real life and not a movie. You don't get a second chance.

So, here's what it boils down to: Are you going to dream or are you going to live? Actually, you can do both. Believe in yourself, put your faith in God and you will accomplish everything you set out to do. If you work, God will work it. Stop holding yourself back and live your dreams!!

BIO

Arnita R. Craighead is an empowerment speaker and CEO of The Motiv8ing Factor. Founded in 2017, The Motiv8ing Factor is focused on mental health wellness, suicide prevention and survival. Arnita is dedicated to living out her purpose of helping to empower others. Her zest for life and gift of gab allows her to deliver her messages in an engaging and relatable manner. While the seriousness of the topics she tackles would make most people uncomfortable, Arnita's candor, sincerity and understanding helps her connect with her audiences and puts them at ease.

Arnita holds a Bachelor's degree in Corporate Communications from Queens College, an MBA with dual concentrations in Entrepreneurship and Leadership & Organizational Management from Georgia State University and is a Certified Life Coach. She resides in Frisco, TX and in her spare time loves to travel, read, cook and spend quality time with those she loves.

DREAM, PLAN, DO, BE - UNICORNS AND TIARAS WHERE TO START TO LIVE YOUR DREAM

By Sally Duxfield

I've often suffered from illusions of grandeur. Well, in my mind I'm terribly important. I know I have things that add value to people's lives. Deep down I know I'm special. But how do I let others know about my 'thing' that's special? Do you wonder how to find your voice too? Do you feel the same, but...? There's that 'but,' right? That little, tiny piece of you that says, "Hey, girl. Who do you think you are?" It might have been something mama said, maybe a teacher, or perhaps even a partner, but the 'but' has lingered. I believe it's in all of us, which is why sharing how we kicked our 'buts' is so vital for us women.

I'm quite old now, and I don't have time to muck around. There are no longer any 'buts' in my vocabulary. Once I chose to put on my tiara and chase down my unicorns, the realization that I was worthy became abundantly clear. As an ex-military officer, owner of my consultancy, an outdoor center, and having just built my own Village (Arete. nz) based in New Zealand, knowing that I've achieved success is clear.

So, how did I kick my own 'but'?

I don't want to just tell my story. I want you to have a road map after all is said and done. Your job in all of this is to get out your pencil and start writing as we walk together.

Note 1 | It Starts With a Dream; Start High Level

You may know the saying, "A dream without a plan is just a dream." This saying is credited to Antoine de Saint Exupéry (1900-1944), and then used in a similar manner by Dale Carnegie in 1976! And it's relevance is absolutely true today. Denzel Washington: Dreams Without Goals Are Just Dreams | Tear-Jerking Speech - YouTube

Task A | Articulate Your Dream/Passion

> Get a huge flip chart (ginormous piece of paper), grab some colored pens, and start smashing out every crazy idea that comes into your beautiful, passionate mind. All of it. No judgement. We are looking for the 30000 foot overview.

Task B | Define your Unicorn (Dream); Go Deep

> Gather a small tribe of other fabulous women whose role is to challenge your assumptions and make you really chew through the pros and cons of your idea--the costs, time frames, who, how, when, where and your why. My advice is for you to go deep and narrow. Choose one or two things that could melt your friends' ears off when you're speaking with fire in your belly about your dream (your unicorn).

Note 2 | Learn to Plan

Planning is the absolute key to kicking your 'but'. My IMPACT-4Q Model was the result of many years of thought leadership and deep thinking. Not only does planning control stress, but it reduces over-whelm, lines up all of your ducks into a gorgeous waggly row, and helps you identify where to start. And start you must!

My latest big, hairy, audacious unicorn dream was to build my own luxury off-the-grid retreat for my leadership clients. I dreamed it to be a space with no wifi and no outlets to recharge devices. It would be a place of extraordinary beauty, but one that was carbon neutral and elegant for refocusing, recharging and refreshing.

Well, there wasn't a spare million dollars in my pocket, but there was *something*. The outdoor center and my consultancy provided a steady source of operational funds, but I had to walk in absolute faith that I was being supported by my husband, my staff, and of course, spiritu-ally. My friends, family and staff thought I was stark raving bonkers... several sandwiches short of a picnic.

Hmph! I wedged that tiara down on my head, flipped my flipchart, made sure my unicorn was in sight, and then laid out a 24-month building project (not a budget, just the project) from gardening and pathways, to a trip to Bali to buy furniture and bedding and right on down to the stunning Italian wood fires that were imported. Did I know the whole budget? No. Did I know where I was going to find the funds? No. Did I know if I was going to succeed? Abso-blimming-lutely! Why? Because I had a plan and faith.

Note 3 | Just Start

Just like eating an elephant, choose which end to begin with and take one bite at a time. You can rejig your course once you've set sail, but you can't reach your destination if you're still tied up in port, suffering from inaction. Choose one or two things to do and start there, prefera-bly in an order that makes sense. But, if you have to start somewhere a little illogically because of lack of funds or knowledge, that's okay too.

Note 4 | Tick It Off

You must have a checklist. Allocate chunks of your time, uninter-rupted, to allow deep thinking and to redefine your plan. Hang that first mind-map session on the wall so it's in front of your face every day. This is science. Seeing your dream and ticking off your list triggers the release of a fabulous bunch of neuro chemicals that increase satisfaction, increase your desire to do it again tomorrow, and let you sleep at night knowing that you're on the pathway.

Arete Retreat. Four years in the dreaming, three years in the planning, two years in the doing, and now I can sit with my tiara slightly askew with a delicious lemon gin in my hand, and be. Was it easy? Heck no! Will I rest on my laurels? Heck no! Is there more? Sure is!

What's next? Reflect.

What would I do more of? What would I do less of?

Reassess. Reapply.

Dream. Plan. Do. Be.

Your turn.

BIO

Sally Duxfield is an industry leader in the art of experiential architecture, designing and delivering transformational leadership coaching and programmes to inspire change. Sally's 30+ years' experience spans a career in the New Zealand Defence Force as the director of her own leadership consultancy, the owner of Makahika Outdoor Pursuit Centre, situated in the Horowhenua, and the founder of one of Aotearoa's first truly off grid, sustainable, luxury retreats, Arete Retreat.

Sally has released a book, *Dream, Plan, Do, Be,* a succinct how-to book written for busy people who want to learn how to reduce stress, decrease anxiety and overwhelm, and gain control of their busy lives. Her planner, Plan It. Do It., is the perfect accompaniment. Her most recent project was the release of her IMPACT-4Q model, a planning model supported by the neuroscience of high performance. The model will be accompanied by a book to be released in 2022.

Website: www.sallyduxfield.com

FROM FOSTER TO FORTUNE: THE POSSIBILITIES ARE UNLIMITED

By Tonya Fairley

Imagine walking into your home, only 12 years old, and being met by a blow so hard that your body goes numb when you hit the floor. Imagine struggling to get up and being met by another blow; this time, your head hits the floor and your nose starts to bleed. Now imagine laying there in a pool of blood trying to figure out what just happened only to open your eyes and see that the person who put you in this position is none other than the woman who gave birth to you. Your Mother. Imagine that as you lay there on the floor, she stands over your body telling you she wishes you were dead and that she hates you. As you lay there in a pool of your own blood with your ears ringing, your younger sibling is crying for help. You are helpless and your body feels lifeless.

One may wonder how you recover from such a tragic experience at such a young age. How do you begin to put the pieces together when they fell apart at the hands of the one God assigned to protect, nurture and care for you?

Often, I would ask myself how in the world could God allow such a tragic event to take place? Why would God allow a child to continue to endure such a life instead of being able to enjoy their childhood? This incident changed the trajectory of my life. Being placed in the foster system immediately following this event made me feel that the world was full of evil and wickedness.

However, I soon learned that it was just the beginning of a life destined for greatness. Often as a young child people would assume the type of person I would become because of the sins of my mother. She was a teenage mom, drug addict, and did whatever she needed to do to make ends meet. She never provided the love one would expect from a mother raising a young daughter. Instead, she was full of anger, rage, and self hatred, and no one encouraged her to get help. So, how could I see greatness you may ask? Well, I didn't but someone else did.

My social worker told me that I was "destined for greatness." I just needed to believe it. I was destined for greatness. I just needed to change my attitude and believe in myself. I needed to know that everything I had been through up until that point was building and shaping my life for something greater than I could imagine.

When I started to believe in myself, my attitude began to change. I began to attract people that had my best interest at heart. I began to feel the people around me pouring into my soul, and nurturing my spirit beyond my understanding. When I started believing in myself, the possibilities of what my life could look like and would be like became *unlimited*. I began to see the unlimited potential that my life's light could bring to others. I began to believe in *Unlimited Possibilities*. I began to believe I could go anywhere, do anything, and help others along my journey.

As I lived through the foster care system, I understood I was not there for just me. I was there to help others live a life of abundance and riches that had nothing to do with money, but everything to do with self-love and determination. From that journey into adulthood, I understood that I was rich in my soul. That was more important than money.

When you understand your calling in life, you understand that everything is possible if you just transform your thinking. You have a clear vision that you can have it all regardless of what you have gone through because the *Possibilities are Unlimited.*

BIO

Tonya Fairley is a globally renowned giant in the Leadership and Business World. She has a 5-Step formula to help business leaders achieve a highly profitable business, and dream life.

Leveraging her 25 years of business experience, Tonya teaches the new age and new way of *Transformational Thinking*, a business owners roadmap to immediately achieve revenue results while living life on their terms.

Her sought after *You Can Have It All Methodology* is a game-changer that has revolutionized companies by transforming their employee mindset and boosting morale, resulting in higher employee productivity, more satisfied customers, and increased profits for the company.

Tonya has a passion for helping great leaders become amazing leaders, while helping them build a winning team culture so their company can fulfill their mission while exceeding customer expectations.

Tonya Fairley is the CEO and Founder of Root Success Coaching and Strandz Unlimited™ Inc (Beauty Supply and Hair Studios). She is also a best-selling author, speaker, and coach.

MARK OF AN ANGEL

By Robin Fortner

My mom was the best friend I didn't even realize I had, and needed. Life experiences have a funny way of testing you. At the age of 21 years old, I took my hardest test.

I thought she would be around forever. We were making plans for the future. I was already thinking about what I wanted to do for her 50th birthday. Little did I know God had a different plan: she wouldn't even live see 47.

I remember the day she passed. A few months prior, she had agreed to participate in a Home Box Office (HBO) documentary about being a hospice patient. At the time, I will admit that I did not understand what hospice really meant. My brother and I held onto faith and believed that she would pull through. She was getting weak; the cancer was eating at her body and organs. There was literally nothing we could do to stop the inevitable. During her last filming session with the hospice staff, it became apparent to us that it would only be a matter of time.

I stood outside her bedroom, listening to the conversations around her. She could barely move her limbs and rarely spoke a word. I started to go in and stop the filming, but I reminded myself that she really wanted to see this to the end…always a fighter. So I simply cried to myself and listened. After all of the cameras were gone and everyone had returned to their own lives, it was often just her and me. I would clean her up and prepare her for the evenings. That night was different. She had a faint smile on her face as she watched me move about in silence. She didn't have enough strength to formulate a word, but I knew she wanted to speak. I remember purposely diverting my eyes from hers. I just couldn't.

As I lowered her back onto the bed, she held me as tight as she could, but was barely holding on. I felt every bit of love through her gentle touch as I positioned her just right. When I raised myself up, she lifted her hand up to grab onto mine, forcing me to look up into her eyes. Oh she knew what she was doing, and I knew to obey. It was in that moment that I realized she was ready, even if I wasn't. I began to weep. For what seemed like a long time, we just looked at each other in silence; more like she watched while I tried to maintain my composure. Finally I told her that I wasn't ready, that I was scared, and I didn't want to lose her. She smiled, reaching up slowly to wipe my tears. I asked her, if she could, would she be my guardian angel. She mustered up enough strength to nod her head and utter, even if in a whisper, YES! Those would be the last words we ever spoke to each other. I sat next to her a little while longer. Her eyes closed soon after.

I was in a very dark space for some time afterwards, upset with life and with God.

My mother was a Christian woman, a praying woman. I had not come to terms with her passing away, and more importantly I didn't understand why God would let this happen to one of His believers. I was ready to give up. I could not enjoy the roses in life for the thorns I chose to see. Nothing seemed possible, or worth it.

After a year of emptiness, I decided to get a tattoo in her honor. As the artist began to draw my tattoo, she recognized a birthmark in the vicinity of where I wanted my tattoo. "Wow," she said, "you have a beautiful birthmark. It looks like an angel…praying." I had never recognized this glob of pigmentation as any particular shape, much less an angel. I couldn't wait for her to finish so I could see. Sure enough, my birthmark had taken the form of an angel. I was reminded of the last words I spoke to my mother and her promise to me. I could hear my mother say rise up Robin, I did not raise you to quit. I had mourned so deeply to myself for so long. I began to understand how our mindsets matter. The way I processed my adversity was destroying me. Suddenly, I did not feel alone anymore. My mother worked too hard for me not to be great.

My mother did not go to college, although she wanted to, so I made sure I finished school and am now in pursuit of my doctorate.

My mother never owned her own home, so I made sure that I owned property in different states to hand down to the next generation and create a legacy.

My mother never invested a dime, and barely was able to save, so I made sure that I educated myself in creating a diverse portfolio. We never have to worry about tomorrow.

My mother never owned her own business and worked tirelessly to make a living, so after serving my country, I made sure that I owned my own LLC and could create my own destiny.

My mother never had a chance to see all of her beautiful grandchildren, so I make sure that I keep her legacy alive and they know her name.

What I thought was impossible was made possible and still the possibilities are limitless, if only I believe. Since then, I remind myself of this story, and have shared it with some others who express tragedy, hoping that in some small way it gives them inspiration and light. I will forever bear a mark of an angel, letting me know my guardian angel is always with me. I am not perfect by any means. All that I am or ever hope to be, I owe to my angel, MOM.

BIO

Robin Fortner is an award-winning inspirational speaker, entrepreneur and leadership development coach. As a Marine Corps veteran, she has been "battle tested" in every facet of life for the last 30 years defining her confidence, power, and resilience as a proven "warrior leader."

Professionally, Robin has always used her voice to impact others and influence change. As a dynamic speaker, Robin commands the room and leaves an indelible mark from the moment she walks in. As founder of RC Fortner Enterprises, her mission is to help organizations develop better leaders and build "resilient teams". Her passion and her energy inspires the audience to manifest their own greatness, revealing inner strengths and warrior qualities. Robin is committed to spreading her message of empowerment through compelling storytelling and sharing her life experiences. She believes that a winning mindset overcomes any challenge.

Website: www.rcfortner.com

Follow me on social media @rcfortner

REACH OUT AND GRAB YOUR POSSIBILITIES

By Dr. Chere M. Goode

I can vividly recall having a dream as a very small child, around the age of 5, of becoming a nurse. I used to dress up for career days in elementary school in all white with my mother's stethoscope around my neck and her nurse's cap on my head. It was a dream that never went away. It grew like a wildfire within my soul and came to reality when I turned 17 years old. You may say, "All kids dream, so what's the big deal?" Well, growing up in poverty in the projects of Baltimore City where very few dream or even know how to dream, hope was low. Many did not even have hopes of making it out of the projects successfully. Drug activity and crime was rampant. Merely going outside to the playground was taking a risk. Many of the youth that grew up in my neighborhood are now deceased. Never did I imagine that becoming a nurse at the age of 17 and now being a nurse for more than 30 years would catapult me into owning three wellness businesses and becoming a 10-time best-selling international author and wellness speaker. The skills nursing has given me allows me to be effective in my body contouring business--*Make Me Over Wellness*, where I'm changing lives by boosting the self-esteem of others.

I *Make Me Over Wellness* afraid in the middle of a pandemic, so don't dare say what's impossible. Take all excuses out of why you cannot reach your dreams. When you explore all the unlimited possibilities available in this lifetime, your mindset shifts. You begin to adopt a winner's mindset. You get more determined to never quit and more determined to achieve all the possibilities you dare to dream. My ambitious mindset is attributed to my mother and her upbringing. She has always been a hard worker and displayed resilience even when life dealt her a hand that wasn't always favorable. There is a different type of mindset required when it comes to desiring more, desiring to win, and putting in the necessary work to achieve the unimaginable. You must believe you are unstoppable!

Here are 14 ways to make progress and move closer to reaching your unlimited possibilities:

1. **Dream Bigger**- Dare to dream the unimaginable dream for your life, then dream even bigger. The bigger the better. The bigger, the more possibilities. Once you make those dreams come to reality, dream even more dreams.

2. **Create a Vision Board**- Out of sight out of mind. Keep your dreams and goals in clear view to remind yourself of why you should keep pushing forward.

3. **Educate Yourself**- Do research. Learn your craft. Be so well versed in your craft that when your time comes to perform, you will excel without hesitation.

4. **Surround Yourself with Like-Minded People**- Winners surround themselves with winners. Surround yourself with others who know that reaching the unimaginable is possible. Surround yourself with people who are excelling in the craft in which you desire to be an expert.

5. **Get Used to the Word 'No'**- 'No' merely means 'next opportunity'. Man's rejection is God's protection. 'No' means 'not

now'. It doesn't mean never. Each no gets you closer to your yes.

6. **Maintain Your Focus**- Avoid distractions. Your sacrifices now will pay off in the future as you reach goals. Distractions hinder progress and put your dreams on the backburner.

7. **Talk Positively to Yourself**- Positive self-talk is imperative. If you don't believe you can achieve your goals, no one else will believe it. Speak life into yourself. Talk to yourself as if you have the contract, position, or career you want.

8. **Get an Accountability Partner**- Having an accountability partner keeps you on track to work on your goals and see results. An accountability partner aids you in avoiding distractions. An accountability partner encourages you and reminds you of your why when you get discouraged or lack motivation to keep pursuing your dreams.

9. **Create a Strategic Plan to Reach Your Dreams and Goals**- Without a blueprint or map, you won't get very far. Put your plan in writing. Write down necessary steps to reach your goals. Beside each step write down ways to accomplish that step. In time, you will see your gradual progress and reach those goals.

10. **Just Do It**- Even if you are afraid to make moves towards your dreams, push forward anyway. You must put some skin in the game. Invest in yourself. Get help. Ask questions. Make moves to get closer to your dreams.

11. **Ride the Wave**- As you pursue your dreams, there will be highs and lows. Things will happen to try to deter you from going forward, but if you ride the wave, things will smooth out and the ups and downs will be well worth the trouble.

12. **Don't Be Afraid to Start Over**- A famous person once said, "If at first you don't succeed, try, try again." Without failures, there is no appreciation for the wins. Don't be afraid to try new ways to reach the same goal. If one way doesn't work, try something else. The only real failure is not trying at all.

13. **Celebrate Your Accomplishments**- Every step you make that gets you closer to the finish line is an accomplishment. Celebrate all your wins.

14. **Reach Back and Help Someone Else Reach Their Goals**- When you help others, the doors to more blessings open for you. Your shine is not dimmed by helping others.

Remember, you are in control of your life. When you breathe your last breath, leave this world knowing that you tapped into all your talents and left no possibilities sitting idle on the table. The only thing standing in your way is you.

BIO

Dr. Chere M. Goode is the Founder/CEO of Total Harmony Enterprises, Make Me Over Wellness, and the Jordan Alexander Cofield Foundation Inc. (a 501C3 foundation in honor of her late son). Goode is a mother, caregiver, and the creator of the annual RECHARGE Health, Wellness, and Fitness Expo. Goode has been a Licensed Practical Nurse for over 30 years and is nationally certified in hospice and palliative care. Goode is a ten time #1 Best Selling International Author, Speaker, Wellness Coach, and American Heart & Stroke Association Ambassador/Spokesperson. Known as the RECHARGE Strategist, Goode teaches professional women strategies for self-care to recharge their mental, physical, and emotional batteries for success in life and business through her 8 Recharge Pillars of Self Care. Goodes' teachings also emphasize the importance of self-care to enrich ones' life. She is a wellness guru and is highly respected in her field of expertise.

ALL THINGS ARE POSSIBLE

By Emma Norfleet-Haley

Join me on this traumatic blast from the past that led to me writing this chapter. My "triumph over trauma" led to "my wellness for self actually being for somebody else. Hence, the need to document and share a roadmap to success on how to resolve trauma and live one's best life. A brief experience will be shared to illustrate how ALL THINGS ARE POSSIBLE.

Hmmm…best life. And how would you go about living your best life after trauma? Well, imagine a 5-year-old girl who was routinely awakened by a drunken father's emotional, physical, and on one occassion, a foiled sexual assault against an older sister of the the 5-year-old. Not only did this father try to sexually assault the older sister, but the father also threatened to kill the teen brother for challenging and interrupting his despicable attempted sexual assault. Now, if this story has raised the hairs on your back thus far, hold on to your seat.

This 5-year-old girl's trauma was not yet done, as the heroic brother's challenge and subsequent foil of this despicable attempted sexual assault against his older sister enraged that father all the more. This rage then turned into a deadly threat.

"Stay right there. I'm gonna kill you, you son of a b_t_h."

The 5-year-old girl, the older sister, and the other siblings were led into the safety of the woods by the heroic teen brother. Unfortunately, the safety of the woods was short lived, as the drunken father actually tried to make good on his threat to kill the 5-year-old's teen brother. The drunken father shot bullets into the wooded area where they sought safety. As bullets whizzed past the 5-year-old's ear, she was paralyzed with fear. The heroic brother, once again, came to the rescue. He momentarily bent down and comforted the 5-year-old.

"I got you baby girl. It's gonna be okay."

And okay it was.

As he rose like the phoenix, he took hold of the 5-year-old's hand and dragged her through the woods 2 ½ miles to the safety of their aunt's home.

As the title of this chapter proclaims, ALL THINGS *really* ARE POSSIBLE. For example, eight siblings escaped rounds of bullets as they fled to and through the woods to an aunt's home 2 ½ miles away; a heroic brother in his mid to late teens prevented a drunken father from sexually assaulting his older sister; and the 5-year-old girl grew up to be...wait for it...this chapter's author, who is a victor and survivor, and now a mental health provider!

So, if YOU are questioning whether it is possible to turn "trauma and tragedy into triumph," know and believe ALL THINGS ARE POSSIBLE. This question to others will forever fuel and drive my mission to assist those who have endured trauma by teaching them how to cope with the unresolved effects of it and live their best lives.

The roadmap to success starts with being aware of and willing to remove the trauma mask. Far too often, too many of us walk around pretending and feeling guilty or embarrassed about past trauma, all while living at less than our best. But what happens when you refuse to unmask and deal with your trauma?

Given that trauma can be emotional, physical, sexual, and environmental, masked trauma can lead to symptoms such as denial, repression, sadness, irritation, isolation, nightmares, and flashbacks. These symptoms associated with unresolved trauma can lead to psychiatric disorders such as Posttraumatic Stress, Generalized Anxiety, and Major Depressive Disorders, to name a few.

If you have been traumatized in the past, it is highly recommended that you seek treatment from a qualified mental health professional. In doing so, you are further advised to secure one of four trauma focused psychotherapies: Prolonged Exposure (PE), Cognitive Processing Therapy (CPT), Eye Movement Desensitization & Reprocessing (EMDR), and Trauma-Focused Cognitive Behavioral Therapy (TF-CBT). Trauma-focused psychotherapies provide a safe, secure and therapeutic environment for you to reflect, reject and reset your mind.

Haley's Mind of Care Services, LLC's (HMOCS, LLC) staff offer quality mental health services that include two of the above evidence-based practices. For anyone who lives in the DMV (District of Columbia, Maryland & Virginia), you can contact HMOCS, LLC, an outpatient mental health agency, for a free PTSD screening. Contact HMOCS, LLC if you're ready to turn your **"tragedy and trauma into triumph"** because **ALL THINGS ARE POSSIBLE.**

Agency Website: www.hmocs.org
Agency Email Address: info@hmocs.org
Agency Phone Number: (240) 429-5390
Instagram: @askmsemma
Facebook: facebook.com/emma.norfleethaley

BIO

Emma Norfleet-Haley, PsyD., LCSW, LICSW, LCSW-C, CAMS I is the President/CEO of Haley's Mind of Care Services, LLC. She is a trained mental health trauma expert who, along with her staff, provides evi-denced-based psychotherapies to help clients "triumph over trauma." Emma also facilitates CEU trainings for clinicians needing licensure re-newal. She is a 2x Amazon #1 Best Seller Co-author, having contributed to Dr. Cheryl Wood's *I Am A Victor* (April 2021) and Les Brown and Dr. Cheryl Wood's *You Are Enough* (June 2021), which was also an International Amazon #1 Best Seller. In December of 2021, Emma authored and released her own book titled ***"How to Unmask and Resolve Trauma."***

TO HEAL IS A CHOICE

By Arprentiss Haye

"It's going to be so easy," said no one ever. If they did, they lied to you. Gold gets brighter when exposed to fire, diamonds are formed under high temperature and pressure, and iron sharpens iron. And what does it mean that life is not fair? The truth is most of us have been subject to the consequences of other people's decisions.

It was not fair that my parents divorced when I was four and my biological father abandoned us. It was not fair that the man who married my mom, and adopted me and my younger brother was incapable of genuinely loving us. It certainly was not fair that my first-born son was tragically taken in someone's selfish act of attempted robbery. That is my life in a nutshell. Whoa, that was a lot! Even still, I am aware that others have suffered far worse childhood traumas. I have always been a bright outgoing person, even been called Sunshine. How does the ability to focus on the positive remain? How am I even in my right mind? As much as we lack control over what happens to us, we maintain the power to choose how we respond.

I did not always realize I had a choice. For most of my life, I held on to the narrative my family instilled in me. When my biological father abandoned us, signed away his parental rights, and remarried, we did not hear from him for six years. What's even more painful, my mother, in her own pain, often told me that he did not want me so badly that he helped pay to give us away. My adoptive father, who for all intents and purposes is my dad, was emotionally unavailable, mentally abusive, and just plain mean. As a little girl I felt unlovable.

My reaction to being abandoned by my biological father and mistreated by my dad was to find someone to love me. Sadly, it began with promiscuity in my pre-teen years. As a young woman I spent years going from relationship to relationship. I was on a mission to find "the one". I was a real-life version of *Runaway Bride*. I was a codependent relationship addict. I lost count, but I was on either my fourth or fifth engagement when I hit my bottom. I felt hopeless. A dear friend listened as much as she could and suggested that I seek help from a professional. We laugh about it now, but it was the best thing she could have done. It was not easy. After all, don't only crazy people go to shrinks? I chose to listen and began my healing process through therapy in my late twenties.

My sixteen years in therapy ended when my therapist retired. However, a year later the loss of my stepmom triggered some unresolved childhood trauma. I went into a depression. I once read that depression is anger turned inward. I was angry that after all the work I had done on myself there was still more. I relented and sought help again. This new therapist's approach was one of self-love. Around the same time, I was re-reading the book *The Four Agreements* by Don Miguel Ruiz. The first agreement is 'Be Impeccable with Your Word'. In the book, he directly correlates the ability to do this with your level of self-love. I felt I was right on track.

Elijah was the first to call me mom. Though he was in his early twenties, I still looked for his text letting me know he was safe whenever he stayed out at a friend's house. On the night that changed everything, his text came in at 8:43 p.m. I drifted off to sleep peacefully; all was well in my world. The next morning, my husband and I were making the bed when we caught a glimpse of a news story headline: "3 Shot,

2 Dead in Roswell". It would be hours later when we realized how significant that story was to us.

We heard several loud knocks on the door and questioned each other over who it could be at 10:30 am. We opened the door to two police officers. They began asking questions about Elijah to establish that they had the right home. I finally asked if he was okay to which one officer replied, "He's deceased." Only the grace of God gave me the strength to come off the floor.

In the days, weeks, and months that followed, I could hardly wrap my mind around my new reality. Eight weeks later my mother had a stroke, then passed away six weeks later. How on earth was this fair? To lose my first born and the person who birthed me. It was unreal. Yet I looked at my twelve-year-old and somehow realized that he deserved to have a whole mom. Therefore I was going to be as whole as I could be.

This is where it all came together. Even in the midst of the excruciating pain of loss, I had a choice: to either shrivel up and die, or to heal and honor my son and mom's legacy. Once again, I chose the hard thing, to heal. This time it was about doing the work of processing grief. About a year before I lost my son and mom, I had begun practicing gratitude. One of the many contributors to Louise Hay and Friends' book *Gratitude A Way of Life* said,

> "Love is the power that heals our lives, and love is the power that will ultimately heal this world. Gratitude comes from love. It is the natural expression of a loving heart. Therefore, whenever we express gratitude, we align ourselves with the power that heals us."

So, it all came full circle. We are first loved by the power that created us. We must choose to receive this love, then love ourselves and, as we love ourselves, express gratitude in everything. We must choose to heal.

BIO

Arprentiss Haye is a second time co-author. Her first book collaboration *Look At Me Now* tells the story of how she and twenty others thrived through the pandemic. She received her Bachelor of Arts in Communication from Mercer University. A fitness professional by day, Arprentiss is on a mission to empower women to gain control of their health through mindset, nutrition, and movement. She also shares her story of finding peace after the loss of her son and mom in the same year to encourage others to keep going. An Atlanta native, she enjoys being a basketball mom to her fourteen-year-old son, spending time with her husband, dancing, and reading.

LIVING FULFILLED, INSPIRED AND TRANSFORMED (F.I.T)

By Cheryl Lynn Jones

I've tried, cried, and failed. I've risen, stumbled, and fallen, and I've learned that a spirit infused with passion and purpose is willing to run, crawl or even limp to the finish line or die trying.

Like most entrepreneurs, I realized early in life that denying or ignoring my dreams and my passion is like a bird denying the urge to fly or a fish ignoring the impulse to swim. It's inconceivable.

I once heard a successful man attribute his success to the fact that "no one told me I couldn't fly." This is a profound revelation because it is our fear of flying, falling, and dying that keeps us from fulfilling our life's potential, and it is our fear of pain, change, and failure that keeps us from manifesting and embracing our divine purpose. Living fulfilled, inspired, and transformed (F.I.T.) requires a willingness to fly, to fall, and to die over and over again. It is in the flight, the rise, and the resurrection that the illusions of fear are shattered and truth is erected, and it is in our pain, change, and failure that miracles are birthed, souls are renewed, and dreams grow wings and take flight.

I was in my 20's when I opened up my own publishing company on 5th Ave. in New York City. I did this because no one told me I couldn't. And with uncompromising passion, I set out to contrast the relentless misrepresentation of Black women in mass media. I took on this challenge because no one told me I shouldn't. I woke up every day believing I would succeed because no one told me I wouldn't. After years of bittersweet victories and defeats, I met my moment of truth.

One evening around midnight in the summer of '98, I was in my New York City office, tired, scared, and alone, holding on to a dying publishing business by a shoestring. In my brokenness, I dropped to my knees and cried like a baby. I cried out for mercy. *"How much longer, God? What am I doing wrong?"* Doubt and fear cornered me and told me I was a failure. My heart swelled, oozing feelings of shame, guilt, and frustration. My head pounded with each cry out for mercy. *"How much longer, God?"* I wanted to give up, quit, and walk away, but through my tears, pain, frustration, and fear, my heart became still. Inside my head I was still screaming, but my heart grew still. I was taken aback by the stillness. It was as if time itself was standing at attention and I couldn't help but follow suit. I was captivated by the stillness when a voice spoke to me and said, "Have I ever let you down?" Through my tears, I answered aloud, *"No, God. You have never let me down."*

"Have you ever prayed for anything that you have not received?"

Through my tears, I answered aloud, *"No, God. I've never prayed for anything that I have not received."*

"Then why would now be any different? I am the same God that has brought you this far. The same God. Trust."

At that moment, through the pain and tears, a calmness swept over me, and I knew that no matter what the outcome,I would be alright. It didn't have to be what I thought it was going to be, but I knew that whatever the outcome, it would be right. At that moment, I chose God.

Since that summer of '98, I followed new dreams, experienced new victories, faced new obstacles, cried new tears, and embraced it all, understanding that my ability to love and accept myself through every stage and phase of my journey is one of the keys to living F.I.T.

Now, as a fitness industry leader, creator of a national fitness brand, and owner of one of the leading fitness studios in Arizona, I can say with certainty that when we are willing to fly, fall and be resurrected, our fear will shatter and truth will prevail, and when we embrace the pain, change and falls in our lives, miracles are birthed, our souls are renewed, and our dreams will grow wings and take flight.

There are many keys to the F.I.T. Formula. I've provided one of my favorite master keys to help you on your path to living fulfilled, inspired, and transformed!

Master Key #1 - *Find the Victory in the Fall*

Our mind is a muscle. Just as we exercise our physical bodies to ensure strength and vitality, exercising our mental muscle to strengthen our minds and sharpen our thoughts is essential to living F.I.T. In short, a weak mind leads to weak actions.

Learning how to find the victory in the fall is one of the ways to begin building your mental muscle and start opening your path to a F.I.T. life.

Find the Victory in the Fall – The Exercise

We often cling to the memory of the "falls" in our lives instead of clinging to the victories the falls created. Memories of past mistakes or failures, if not positively assessed, can immobilize us and hinder our exploration, expression, and willingness to move forward. Make a list of the things you thought were failures in your life. Take some time to review each incident and identify the good things that evolved from each of them. Perhaps your fall made room for a special person to enter your life or provided a valuable lesson that assisted you later in life. Perhaps it shifted you to a new location or career path or provided you with an opportunity to help someone else in need. Disciplining ourselves to finding victory in the fall is one of the keys to living fulfilled, inspired, and transformed.

BIO

Cheryl Lynn Jones is a fitness expert and owner of one of the leading fitness studios in Arizona. She was the center-stage fitness feature at the ESSENCE Festival for two consecutive years and has been featured in *ESSENCE, Channel 3TV's Good Morning Arizona, Sirius XM's Karen Hunter Show* and *News One Now* with Journalist Roland Martin.

Cheryl is also the creator of the *Rhythm Rumble Workout*, a unique exercise system that has globally impacted the fitness industry and combines dance and martial arts for the most fun you will ever have while exercising. Cheryl has partnered with industry leaders such as *Black Enterprise, Lisa Nichols and Dr. George Fraser* and continues to push fitness into unchartered territory. She was recently invited to West Africa to utilize her branded workout in a Global S.T.E.A.M project targeting Ghanian teenage girls in engineering.

Website: www.rhythmrumble.com

IG @rhythmrumbleworkout

FB @Rhythmrumbleworkout

MSA FORMULA: GET WHAT YOU WANT IN LIFE AND BUSINESS

By Dr. Karen Lewis

Do you wish you could wave a magic wand to get to the level where you know you should be in life and business? Though I don't have a magic wand, this formula I'm sharing with you is about as close as you can get.

I'm grateful every day that I have the luxury of providing financially for my family, giving support to my legally blind husband, caring for my elderly mother, and saving generously for retirement, all while working *on* my business, rather than the stress of working *in* the business.

I gotta take you back in history so I can really share my drama on the road to the manifestation of my dream. I have over 30 years of business experience. The biggest pitfall entrepreneurs fall into is getting so caught up in their business, that they end up landing in one of these two categories: In a burnout, or on their way to it.

Imagine a stadium that holds 50,000 people. Now imagine that about 15,000 of them do not show up. The rest of the seats are taken. The seats that are taken hold the percent of entrepreneurs that deal with burnout day in and day out.

There was a time when I lived in a tiny shoebox apartment, surviving paycheck to paycheck, wishing, and dreaming for something more. My tiny apartment smelled of sweet strawberries, but was furnished with a mattress so small that my feet used to hang over the edge. From that mattress, I could reach the dresser, the wall opposite the bed, and my bathroom door. While living in that little Barbie shoebox apartment, I was doing something I loved, but I was broke! I was 36 years old, feeling hopeless, stuck, and too old to have a single quarter in my saving's jar. I cried for days; I had to do something different! I was burnt out, but not completely disgusted with myself.

A friend in real estate inspired me. Those big checks she made were the real deal, and they kept coming. It was one hot morning in sunny south Florida, while sitting in my Barbie shoebox apartment with that one quarter in the jar, that I decided real estate was my future. I too wished for that magic wand but knew if real estate was meant to be, it was up to me.

Today, I own a real estate brokerage firm with 50 agents, and our sales increase every year; my company is on the rise. I'm being headhunted by one of the top brokerage firms in the country. I no longer live paycheck to paycheck, and I can provide for my family, set aside funds for retirement, breathe easy, and not burn out. I have the freedom to work *on* my business and not have to work *in* my business.

Yes, I went through trials and tribulations and ups and downs, but through my struggle I discovered the MSA formula that works every single time. I'm glad to share it with you, so you can reach your goals sooner, quicker, and faster.

M – Mindset

To achieve new goals, you must first change your *Mindset*. The mindset *must* be changed. Once the Mindset changes, your thought process changes, and then you start changing your belief system.

I had several beliefs that I had to change in order to achieve the things I have. I had to surrender and finally disconnect from negative people in my life—some were even family members. I started reading and associating with the right people. It wasn't easy, but as hard as it was, it had to be done. You can do it, too.

S – Skill set

You must have the *Skills*. It's important to have a skill set because you don't want to have to chase people. When you have the right skill set, people will come to you.

I had a new agent on our team that was struggling. I taught her the MSA formula and helped her develop new skills. She went from being broke and busted to vacationing in Italy, having a second home, and homeschooling her children. She is on track to earn $200,000 this year. She developed her Mindset, her Skill set, and took Action to get results!

A – Action

You get results when you take *Action*. There is easy access to all kinds of information, especially on the Internet. If you don't implement action, you're not going to get the results. LeBron James bounces that ball day in and day out. He is perfecting his skill set. He is in action.

MSA Formula to get you in Action and get results!

1. Write an affirmation 21 times for 21 days.

I wrote my affirmation, pen onto paper: I enjoy recruiting five agents per month. I wrote it 21 times for 21 days. I exceeded my goal and happily recruited 13 agents in a month.

2. Gain new skills and grow.

The simplest, fastest way to do this is by following mentors online. Oprah Winfrey and Les Brown for example share good quality content. You can also follow me @drkarenlewis for daily inspiration, business info, real estate tips, and more. Let's connect!

3. Take action.

I'm going to cheer you on and hold you accountable. Maybe your next action is to apply for your real estate license. Maybe your next action is to open that business. Whatever it is, when you discover it, tag me on social media. Use the hashtag #befree2022 so I can find you. I want to support you, and I want to cheer you on.

BIO

Dr. Karen Lewis is a licensed real estate broker at K1 Realty Group, LLC. located in South Florida. She is also licensed in Georgia. She has a passion for sharing golden nuggets to help real estate agents all over the country succeed. Dr. Karen is a member of the National Association of Real Estate Brokers, certified instructor with Florida Realtors, real estate instructor with Victory Real Estate School, Broward-Miami ambassador, and the president of Aim to Achieve, not-for-profit organization.

Dr. Karen is also the Host of "The Real on Real Estate Radio Show." She has more than 30 years of experience in business. She has worked in management, overseen mentoring programs, hosted television shows, facilitated empowerment trainings, edited monthly newsletters, and published a teen magazine. She has also conducted many workshops, webinars, and done coaching and consulting work. Dr. Karen has been blessed with a wide variety of life experiences.

IG handle: @drkarenlewis

THE COURAGE TO HAVE UNCOMFORTABLE CONVERSATIONS

By CheVaughn Mack

"For God has not given us a spirit of fear, but of power and of love and of a sound mind."

2 Timothy 1:7 (NKJV)

All relationships require work, but the work doesn't *have* to be hard. See, many of us have been conditioned to believe that if we want something good in life, especially a good romantic relationship, we have to endure a bunch of heartache and pain before that's even possible. Well, I'm here to tell you that that is a lie! Not only do you *deserve* the relationship of your dreams, you are capable of creating the relationship of your dreams! It all starts with effective communication, and in particular, your ability to have uncomfortable conversations with your partner. Now, if you believe your relationship is already too far gone or that either one of you is too set in your ways to be able to talk candidly with one another and get a positive outcome, I invite you to take a few moments before you read any further and ask God to partner with us as I guide you on a journey to help take your relationship from merely surviving to thriving, one conversation at a time.

In your own words, pray to God about the following: (1) Ask God to be in the center of this journey as we touch on an uncomfortable topic. (2) Ask God to give you and your partner peace that surpasses all understanding. (3) Ask God to tear down anything in the relationship that does not have a foundation built on Christ. (4) Ask that God would rebuild the relationship on His Word. (5) Dedicate your relationship to Him and ask Him to direct both your and your partner's paths, in Jesus' name. Amen!

There are so many reasons that people find it difficult to communicate effectively with their partners. Sometimes we are so focused on getting our point across that we become selfish during the conversation and forget (or refuse) to listen to our partners when they talk back to us. Other times, we end up listening to our partners in order to respond to them instead of listening to understand them.

I've found that more often than not, we avoid having uncomfortable conversations with our partners because we fear their response. Now, that fear is usually not apparent to us. In fact, we might not even recognize it as fear because it often comes with several layers of "stuff" beneath it. Buried beneath the fear of our partners' response is our desire to control them. Unbeknownst to us, we attempt to try and control our partners' actions and responses by refusing to talk about anything that will cause *us* to experience unwanted emotions. And buried even further beneath control are unaddressed issues, and maybe even some trauma. The reason that we don't recognize these things as fear is because it disguises itself as other things like wanting to keep the peace in the home or a desire to stop arguing with each other so much.

Now that we've exposed fear, control, and unaddressed issues, let me guide you through a very practical, yet extremely powerful way to help you start a conversation about expectations. This topic is very necessary, yet it can be the uncomfortable conversation you've been avoiding. When you're ready to get started, grab a pen and paper and respond to the following prompts. The key to the exercise is to be honest with your answers and courageous enough to later discuss them with your partner. You can use this exercise as a template for other uncomfortable conversations you need to have.

Expectations

Having unspoken expectations of your partner and the relationship can cause turmoil if not addressed. Oftentimes we enter into relationships with unspoken expectations, and we have the nerve to get upset when those unspoken expectations are not met. That stops today! My prayer is that by the end of this exercise, uncomfortable conversations will turn into common conversations for you and your partner. I must warn you, though, that it's going to take some effort and consistency on your part to see positive results.

Exercise

- Write a detailed list of the expectations you have for your partner.

- Write a detailed list of the expectations you have for your relationship.

- Write a detailed list of the expectations you have for yourself.

- How long have you had these expectations?

- Have your expectations changed over time? Why or why not?

- Are you aware of your partner's expectations of you and the relationship?

- If so, what are they?

- If not, why are you not aware of those expectations?

- After you began writing, did anything on the lists surprise you?

- Why or why not?

- Is your partner aware of your expectations of them and the relationship?

- What has stopped you from sharing your expectations with them?

Action: Pray 2 Timothy 1:7, then share your answers with your partner. Encourage your partner to complete the exercise and share their answers with you.

BIO

CheVaughn is the founder and CEO of The Word Perspective, LLC, a coaching and consulting company that offers couples coaching and group coaching. She is a Christian relationship strategist who empowers her clients to strengthen their relationships by eliminating unhealthy behaviors through positive communication. She is blessed with a unique perspective and optimistic outlook on relationships, which enables her to teach her clients how to use the power of their words to foster healthy relationships.

Website: www.TheWordPerspective.com

Book A Call: https://TheWordPerspective.as.me/

Follow CheVaughn on Social Media:

Facebook @CoachCheVaughn

Instagram: @TheWordPerspective

GRATITUDE IS MY ATTITUDE AND MY POSSIBILITIES ARE UNLIMITED

By Seanta C. McClendon

"I know what it is to be in need, and I know what it is to have plenty. I have learned the secret of being content in any and every situation, whether well fed or hungry, whether living in plenty or in want. I can do all this through him who gives me strength."

Philippians 4:12-13

As a career minded United States Air Force officer with limitless possibilities, I knew the time would come when I'd have to spend some time serving my country across enemy lines. Being female, I figured I wouldn't necessarily have to don a rucksack, sling a M-16, or live in a foxhole for six months; or at least that was my prayer. My thoughts and fears were partially true; gratefully some of them were false. I was not on the frontline with live rounds of ammunition shooting over my head, not like the times I remember during the drug raids when I was a child growing up in Detroit. Nor did I have to live in a foxhole for six months. I did have to sling a M-16 and become very intimate with my 9mm handgun. I took it with me to bed at night and to the shower in the morning. That was the longest six months of my life. Gratitude was certainly my attitude, and I was counting down the days.

Now don't get me wrong, there were a few minutes a day for leisure and exercise. I even took a few day trips into town. Imagine if you will, a huge mall full of designer stores and crowds of women shopping in silence. That's right. At no time were women allowed to speak in public; not even to each other. On one occasion, my office staff tried to dine together at a local restaurant. However, we couldn't find one where women were allowed to eat on the same side with the men and it clearly wasn't safe for me to dine alone. See, I was the Executive Officer for the 363d Air Expeditionary Wing Commander, at Prince Sultan Air Base, Kingdom of Saudi Arabia. I was also the only female officer on staff. It was my duty to coordinate administrative and operational tasks for over four thousand members in Southwest Asia for three or more countries at a time. And I had to coordinate all of that with the Royal Saudi Air Force.

At the end of every Six-month deployment, there was a big dinner with Wing Commander and his senior staff of high-ranking male officers. This dinner was traditionally hosted by a ranking official of Prince Sultan. This time, for the first time, there was an invitation for the Wing Executive Officer…ME! Executive Officer, that's right I was the first woman ever invited to this official feast. Yes, indeed this created quite a stir all over the base. Personally, I thought I'd hit the lottery. Professionally, I knew I was breaking barriers and creating new possibilities. To be invited to dine with the commanders at the home of a senior ranking member of the Royal Saudi Air Force, gratitude was certainly my attitude. Then I thought to graciously decline. However, that would have caused sheer embarrassment, not only for our military command, but for the entire country. I knew better and I also knew to dress in proper Saudi attire.

When we arrived at what appeared to be a palace, I was immediately directed to the back of the house to chat with three young ladies and a toddler who was playing. This was the wife, two teenage daughters, and a baby son. They were very eager to talk to me. They wanted to know how I felt working with men all day and they had lots of questions about colleges and universities in the United States. My chest was puffed up just thinking about the land of the brave and the free; gratefulness was again oozing out of me. Soon, I was called to dinner. Now let's talk about this feast. Have you ever seen or heard of a "Goat Grab"? It's a celebration dinner in Saudi Arabia where you sit on the floor, criss-cross applesauce, and literally eat everything with your fingers. We had a whole grown goat, a succulent lamb, individual mounds of rice, peas, onions, cucumbers, Arabic bread, and assorted fruit all laid out in front of us.

That feast was an experience to write home about, and I did! We also had dessert and chi on the lanai (hot spiced tea on the patio). I left my camera inside on the chair because I wanted to capture the beautiful bright stars and crescent moon lighting the entire sky. When I went back in the house, into the room where we had devoured that grown goat down to the carcass, my feet were stuck, I mean glued to the rug. What my eyes saw has been pierced in my mind like a tattoo etched on my brain…were his wife and kids really eating our leftovers, the leftover mess we ate with our hands? Every time I tell this story, the hairs on my arms stand straight up and the tears from my eyes fall down.

I was a woman grateful to simply be invited to the royal palace to feast, and the women at the palace were grateful to simply feast on my leftovers. Just as the scripture above, I know what it is to be in need and I know what it is to have plenty. Whether well fed or hungry, whether living with plenty or in want, we must be grateful for it all. I challenge you to an entire day where gratitude is your attitude. I challenge you to look at the stars and crescent moon, and view the vast possibilities that lay in front of you. Gratitude Is My Attitude and My Possibilities are Unlimited!

BIO

Seanta C. McClendon is a retired decorated veteran with over 20 years of military service. Early in her career, she was labeled "The Mentor for all Members". Major McClendon has hung up her military uniform, but not her passion to serve. As the President and CEO of C Life Coach, LLC, she serves as a Mental Motivator and a Chaos Orchestrator. It is her number one mission to get you from where you are to where you desire to be. She is a servant leader who thoroughly enjoys empowering others. She promotes wellness, self-defense, and self-care. She humbly serves her community, church, and family as a human, woman, mother, daughter, sister, speaker, trainer, teacher, coach, manager, mentor, leader, and friend. As a Diamond Life member of Delta Sigma Theta Sorority, Inc., she serves and promotes sisterhood, scholarship, and service!

Websites: clifecoach.net
                     cselfcare.net

Instagram: seantacselfcare

LinkedIn/Facebook: Seanta C. McClendon

IT'S NEVER TOO LATE TO REACH YOUR FULL POTENTIAL

By Eva Medilek

Out of 30 girls accepted to my dental hygiene program, only two were Black, and I was the only one of the two who graduated. One of my instructors told me that I would never be successful as a hygienist. Her words hit me like a challenge. I remember thinking how I would prove her wrong and be one of the most successful hygienists in New York City. Six months later, I was cleaning the teeth of the acting legend, Sidney Poitier. I was on my way.

Actors, actresses, models, and business moguls came to me to whiten their smiles. My boss declared that I was the highest-paid hygienist in New York. It felt good to make it in New York after being told I would never be successful. Then, 9/11 shook the world, and like many, I felt the need to leave New York and find success elsewhere. I moved to San Francisco and started over in my 40's.

I found a job, had a new husband, and life was good. Then, one week shy of my 50th birthday, I was cut, and suddenly I found myself panicked and desperately looking for work to survive. Being in my 50's and going on interviews after 30 years in the profession was humiliating. I knew I was meant for more. I never wanted to need or depend on a job again. I wanted the time and the financial freedom to live the life of my dreams, to travel, and to live anywhere in the world. I knew if I didn't live a life of my choice, I wouldn't be happy settling for mediocrity. It was the kick in the butt I needed to live up to my full potential. I was on a mission to answer the question: *What exactly IS my full potential?*

Going back to school to train for another J.O.B. at my age was not an option. I wanted to be an entrepreneur and work from anywhere in the world. My husband and I had the dream to spend our summers in Europe, but we had no real plans to make it come true. This was all happening so we could realize that dream, but how?

I attended a meeting for network marketers and was gifted the book *Rich Dad, Poor Dad* by Robert Kiyosaki. That book introduced me to real estate investing. After enrolling in a free seminar to learn how to invest in real estate, I realized the possibilities were unlimited. This was it! I could do this! This was the ticket to unlocking my full potential and creating a way to realize our dreams. But that ticket came at a very high-priced investment that included coaches and mentors who would show me how to implement the training in real life so I could be successful. It was worth it!

I maxed out every credit card I had. I was fully committed to making it work. My husband, not so much. I was faced with the choice of betting on my success and risking my marriage or living in mediocrity. It felt as if he thought I couldn't be successful as a real estate investor. I had to fight to prove him wrong. This was my chance to fulfill our dreams.

I traveled to the trainings, studied, researched, and made offers in my spare time while holding down a job. I was doing it all, and I was exhausted. After 6 months, I finally got a deal and my husband was all in. We rehabbed and flipped our first house. It was fun, exciting, and stressful, but worth it. We were now partners in our own real estate investing company. Over the next 3 years, we flipped houses and contracts, held rental properties, and became money lenders. Four years after taking that risk, we were inducted into the Rich Dad Education

Hall of Fame. We also bought our apartment in Berlin, Germany, and I fulfilled my dream of being on HGTV's House Hunters International. I was a successful real estate investor.

Because of my success, I was asked to join the training company as a coach and mentor. It was during my coaching of these aspiring real estate investors that I realized it wasn't just the knowledge of real estate investing that made me successful. It was my mindset, focus, and commitment. Many people had invested in the education and training but never found success.

Here's what I learned on my journey to success:

1. There will always be someone who doubts your ability to achieve your goals. Use that as fuel to keep going.
2. Taking risks requires courage. You can mitigate that risk by getting training and hiring coaches and mentors.
3. Your why has to be bigger than your excuses. Accept that it will be a struggle and stay focused on why you have your goal.

The 3 things that you must establish to build a foundation for your success are:

Clarity – Be clear on what you want and what makes you happy. Be clear on who you are and what's important to you, and live in alignment with that.

Priorities – Establish clear priorities. When your priorities are clear, decision-making becomes easy.

Responsibility – Own the responsibility of creating and setting boundaries so you can stay focused on your priorities. Without boundaries, you end up overcommitted and exhausted.

Your performance and your success come down to the ability to be clear. Prioritize and take responsibility for creating boundaries that support your goals and values. Only then can you realize your full potential.

Who knew that the only Black woman to graduate dental hygiene school in 1980 would become a real estate mogul and a certified high-performance coach after the age of 50? I certainly didn't. It's never too late to reach your full potential. Your possibilities are unlimited. Believe in your greatness, not your limitations.

BIO

Eva Medilek is a certified high-performance coach, international speaker, author, and cultural intelligence trainer. She is a graduate of Ascension Leadership Academy, the High-Performance Institute, and the Certified Master Trainer Program.

Eva is the author of *The Intimacy of Race*: *How to Move from Unconscious Racism to Active Allyship for People of Privilege*. She is the creator of The Intimacy of Race Facebook group, a group that is committed to sharing resources for allies of people of color. An executive contributor to *Brainz Magazine*, Eva was selected as one of 500 people featured on the Brainz 500 Global list of 2020 and 2021.

Eva specializes in helping busy professionals have more money, time, and success without sacrificing health, well-being, and relationships in the process. She shows her clients that it's possible to have it all without having to do it all.

Website: www.evamedilek.com

IG: @evamedilekexecutivecoach

LinkedIn: www.linkedin.com/in/evamedilek/

RISE LIKE THE PHOENIX AND TAKE YOUR NEXT LEAP OF FAITH

By **Saidah Nairobi**

"Be transformed by the renewing of your mind..."

(NIV, Romans 12:2)

Months after giving birth to my second child, I found myself an exhausted mother of two girls, and a frustrated wife struggling to break through a heavy season in my marriage. I was also an overwhelmed creative trying to reinvent myself and my brand throughout different transitions in my career. I barely had any energy left to even think of filling my cup with adequate self-care.

I had taken some massive leaps of faith, which yielded success in both my professional and personal life, so at first it seemed as though I had the strength and endurance to maintain the flight of my journey. Yet, suddenly my feet felt like they'd been cut out from under me. As I tried to catch myself, I looked up and found myself in a valley. I was confused, sad, and felt heavy; it appeared there was no end in sight and no help to bear the weight of my burdens. My mind was scattered.

How did I go from having this fierce determination and momentum to being utterly lost, empty, and unsure of myself?

Well, I am here as a living testimony that there is a light at the end of the tunnel. I am here to implore you to stop doubting yourself. The limitless possibilities of your reality very much still exist. I am here to speak to the light in you that knows that no weapon formed against you shall prosper. And I am here to remind you that weeping may endure for a night, but joy comes in the morning. It is the dawn of a new day. Your morning has come. And it is time to reclaim your strength and stand firm in your power.

Perhaps your inner dialogue has been expressing this desire to push forward in the steps it will take to accomplish new goals. Maybe you've had a vision planted in your heart that is longing to sprout up, but your mental valley is damaging the seed. Every step out of the valley is going to require the ABC approach: *action, belief, and commitment.* Unlimited possibilities await when you are actively committed to believing in the victorious life you are destined to live.

Here are 5 steps to take to renew your mind, rise like the phoenix, and tap into your limitless possibilities.

STEP 1: SAY HELLO TO YOUR SHADOW

In order to live the limitless life you've always wanted to experience, you've got to be transparent, straight, no chaser, and keep it all the way one hundred with yourself. Say hello to your shadow. Evaluate and assess the parts of yourself you've avoided long enough. Explore your patterns, thoughts, and behaviors. It's time to peel back the layers of yourself and take inventory. Where is your mental, emotional, and spiritual supply well stocked? Where are they empty? What has expired? What's been tucked away that needs to come off the shelf and onto display?

The more willing you are to surrender your mask, the more capable you are of resisting limitations in your life.

STEP 2: FORGIVE

Forgiveness is the foundation that allows us to truly let go. If we want to get our mind out of the valley, we have to get our heart out of the gutter. The root of our problems arise from judgement of others and their behaviors as well as judgement of self. If we come to step number two and there is resistance from within surrounding forgiveness, then it's time to go back to step one and do additional uprooting. In order to graduate past step two and be fully engaged in your active belief and commitment to your limitless possibilities, forgiveness is a must step. If we wholeheartedly give ourselves and others the grace it takes to forgive, we launch a rocket of healing that fills every space within that most vital organ.

STEP 3: LET GO

Holding on to the burdens of yesterday make today heavy, and to-morrow unbearable. It's time to release the dead weight. There are several ways to approach this step, but my favorite practice of letting go is writing down on a sheet of paper every low vibrational thought or action that I identified while taking self-inventory.

Also write down every person and more importantly, the experience surrounding that person or group of persons that led to a hardening of the heart and the consequential inability to forgive. This step is a cleanse. We are cleansing our mind and energy fields of the old, and making room for the new empowering, inspiring, transformational, motivating, and edifying thoughts, actions, and experiences that we greatly deserve.

STEP 4: PRAY, MEDITATE, CELEBRATE

Now that we've completed the heavy lifting in the first three steps, it's time to seal that deep purifying work with spiritual intimacy. This step is a means of support as you rehabilitate your mind to actively believe and commit to your limitless possibilities. Scripture says rejoice always, pray without ceasing, and give thanks in all circumstances. There is a reason that rejoicing, prayer, and gratitude are linking chains. This is your ABC approach in spiritual form. As you take your next step with a lighter mind and heart, your temple and spirit are also lighter and ready to support this renewed you. So pray over your victory, meditate on the goodness of life, and make a joyful noise because your best is yet to come.

STEP 5: AFFIRM, BELIEVE, CLAIM and RECEIVE IT

Your unlimited possibilities are right at the top of this step. Affirm it. Your unique mark on life comes with an identity exclusive to you. Believe it. Your strength, endurance, power, momentum, sustainability, joy, peace, prosperity, and favor are here for the taking. Claim it. And should you ever need a refresher on affirming, believing, and claiming your greatest chapter yet, surround yourself with like-minded individuals and immerse your soul in a community that ignites and supports your brilliance and evolution.

Your phoenix has risen. You are ready to take a new leap of faith and soar. Unlimited possibilities are here. Receive it.

BIO

Saidah Nairobi, an Atlanta native by way of Queens, NY, is an author, speaker, licensed realtor, actor, singer, and mentor, but she is most widely known as a professional dancer that blazed stages across the globe with musical icons such as Beyonce (I Am World Tour, Formation World Tour), Usher (OMG World Tour), Ciara, and Ne-Yo. Her dance memoir, *Leap of Faith: The Journey of A Dream* speaks on Saidah's unorthodox journey from aspiring performer to becoming an inspirational globally touring dancer.

Saidah is passionate about mentoring young women in her community, and believes unwavering faith and full confidence in the gifts and talents uniquely given to us is key to unleashing the highest potential of our purpose. Saidah resides in ATL with her husband, two daughters, and their poodle. You can stay in touch with Saidah by following her on social media @saidahnairobi. Autographed copies of Leap of Faith are available to order at www.leapoffaithmemoir.com.

POSSIBILITIES UNLIMITED WITH LOVE-N-HOPE

By Withza L. Nibbs

My name is Withza L. Nibbs, and like many of you, I am made up of **Triple Threats**: *Trials, Tribulations, and Traumas.* Overcoming my triple threats has allowed me to *Triumph* in life. According to the Merriam-Webster dictionary, a *Triple Threat* is a person proficient in three essential skills with a particular field. My experiences made me a better person, and today my life represents possibilities unlimited **With Love -N- H.O.P.E. *(Have Only Positive Expectations)*.**

How did I get here?

As I look through the rear-view mirror reflecting on my life's journey, I can remember the **Trials**, **Tribulations,** and **Traumas** that came along with being an African Haitian immigrant migrating to America. Based upon the narratives, they were told by others who made the journey before them. My parents left everything back in Haiti as they too took the journey searching for a better life. For example, unlike Haiti, electricity runs 24 hours a day with "No power outage," and the grocery stores are always stocked in America. They failed to mention that you must work hard and the **Trials** to pay the electric company and have the luxury to shop at the grocery stores. Although the journey of traveling to a place that you are known as an Alien was painful and, at times, even felt unbearable, making the transition one of the most humbling times of my life. I will forever owe my parents a debt of gratitude for wanting better and pursuing a life of unlimited possibilities.

As a result of my childhood trials, I became an adult who had a heart for serving and advocating for those who were less fortunate than me. My education and my life experiences molded my character to demonstrate the qualities of a servant leader. God has equipped me with the skills necessary to relate to immigrant children and families. My passion for serving others has brought me both pleasure and **Tribulations**. While on the path to becoming a great servant leader, it became evident that the more I helped people, the more I became a target for jealousy, envy, and betrayal. The most painful realization was that it was coming from among close family members and friends.

"Till death, due us part" is what I vowed when I married my husband. Those words were tested when my husband of 24 years took a *"Plead of Convenience,"* which took him away from his family for eight years. I was **Traumatized**. Suddenly, I found myself living the life of a *"Single Parent"* and being the *"Wife of an Inmate."* I was angry and stubborn. I did not want to hear what anyone had to say, but I wanted everyone to listen to me. Throughout the court hearings, God revealed all intentions and the root of the attack. I had to stop asking God, *"Why me?"* One day, he responded and said, *"Why not you?"* I had to lean not unto my understanding and remain in faith, allowing God's will to lead me to *Possibilities unlimited* **with Love -N- H.O.P.E.**

Nevertheless, God got my attention during the Pandemic 2020; I learned to mute myself, took a **"Q.T.I.P.,"** Quit Taking It Personal, listened twice, and moved in silence. The more I became silent, the more the right people supported me. Serenity surrounds my family and me. I was confident, and the battle was God's. People were confused about my silence when I had total control of my emotions by saying to myself, **"Not Now."** I did not invest in the negative, despairing, deceitful conversations taking place "**No comment**," only "**Forgiveness**." I became humble, grateful, elated, and honored for having the power to listen, to inspire others from God, nature, and *Triple Threats* life experiences. I learned that being a thoughtful listener, choosing words carefully, being patient, reflecting, and forgiving myself and others brings serenity **with Love -N- H.O.P.E.**

All in all, I have gained the power to be proficient in dealing with life's Triple Threats. I lead **with Love -N- HO.P.E.** as God always places people in our lives who provide us with the knowledge we need to succeed.

As a Servant Leader, I passionately believe that there is happiness in serving others. I am always looking for ways to help those less fortunate in my community. God has placed people in my life to balance my vision of the world. I embrace silence which brings confidence as a woman and a leader. I learn to rely on God, the inner strength of my body and my soul. My faith is what feeds my ambition to serve others. As a leader, I limit self-pity and negative thoughts and actions. I shall continue to lead with *Possibility Unlimited* **with Love -N- H.O.P.E.**

Today, I have accepted my past, supported my present, and encouraged my future as a wife and mother, a daughter, a sister, and forever a learner. I am strong enough to believe in myself, turn dreams into plans, and turn plans into reality, soaring beyond unlimited possibilities. Life is a constant motion of trials, tribulations, and traumas, but through **Love-N-hope**, one can triumph over them all and embrace the unlimited possibilities that are waiting with their name on them and soar. In order to soar, one must demonstrate resiliency and perseverance.

Your **Triple Threats** may have you stuck and stagnate. Unable to move beyond the pain and embrace ….

However, there is no limit to what you can achieve through faith, resilience, and perseverance.

Perseverance is my fuel, my superpower to **Triumph**! I learned to be silent and listen to my cheerful inner voice to make decisions bravely, be driven by determination toward accomplishments, and aim high! It is just a sign of greatness.

It is powerful to reach **Triumph**; that is when possibilities become unlimited; I embraced it and the changes that bring the message of my **Trials, Tribulations, Traumas** to **Triumph.**

My ears are fine-tuned to listen to God's calling to lead with *Possibilities Unlimited* **With Love -N- H.O.P.E.**

BIO

Withza L. Nibbs is a Haitian American woman's advocate. She believes in giving back to her community through **With Love-N- H.O.P.E**. She is a woman of many titles that always looks to help the less fortunate through lending a helping hand. She has received a master's degree in School Counseling with a minor in Mental Health, a bachelor's degree in Social Work, and an education specialist's degree in Marriage and Family/ Substance Abuse. Withza helped teach English as a Second Language at St. Mary's Cathedral Catholic Church in her earlier years. To impact the United States' highest population of recidivism, as a lifetime advocate for mental health and positive mindset, she founded an organization, **With LOVE-N-H.O.P.E. (*Have, Only, Positive, Expectations) L.L.C.*** to support offenders, families, and victims with consulting, coaching, motivation, and counseling through the Pre and Post incarceration process challenges. Follow her @**WLNHOPE100** on **F.B.** and **I.G.**

THERE IS NO TIME LIKE THE PRESENT TO CREATE YOUR FUTURE

By Chineme Noke

How do you feel? Every living day brings its own challenges, many of which cause us to feel put-upon, disregarded, disrespected or just plain wronged.

Major or minor, there are those issues which dominate our minds causing our thoughts to literally spiral out of control, preventing us from moving forward. What if we recognized that it's not actually the people or the situations, **but our own feelings and reactions** to whatever happened that are making us feel sad or bad?

It is for **you** to do whatever is required to deal with your feelings and move forward; otherwise those feelings can consume your waking thoughts, causing anxiety, resentment, or distress which inevitably hinders and limits successful living.

I am offering 7 action steps for taking responsibility for your own wellbeing and creating happier and unlimited possibilities for your future. They are to be utilized in any troublesome situation and are designed to help you change your attitude to the challenges we all encounter in our lives.

I have used these steps on behalf of my daughter who has a profound learning disability, to help her learn to read. I took control of a situation that was causing me much distress and sleepless nights. The public education system had overlooked her inability to read, in contravention of the law which stipulates that every child should receive an education appropriate to **their** particular needs.

For me, the crucial question was, how could I ensure an appropriate level of education for my daughter through the school system? How could I ensure she is taught to read? This problem seemed to consume my very existence and that is why my action steps were formulated.

No matter what the problem may be, it is important that it is effectively dealt with for us to be able to move forward. I did extensive research on **how** my daughter needed to be taught so that I could persuasively present my findings to the Education Authorities.

Our journey was long and very difficult, ultimately requiring legal court action. However it was worthwhile. My success ensured my daughter became a proficient reader. Plus, I have gained a wealth of knowledge, skills and personal experience that can help others. As we go through the 7 action steps, we open ourselves up to all kinds of possibilities and outcomes, and our quest will certainly help our own personal development, growth and well being.

The 7 Action Steps:

Step 1 – Recognize the precise problem/injustice causing your unrest.

In my case, my daughter needed to be taught how to read.

Step 2 – Identify the issues that created the problem or dilemma.

What was the trigger? My daughter has cognitive learning difficulties which were misunderstood or overlooked. At this step, review the big picture and consider whether it is worth pursuing.

Step 3 – Find out which channels you can use to address your issue.

Perhaps an apology, formal complaint, or legal processes could be sought. Whatever you consider the next avenue to be, this step will allow you to re-evaluate the situation and help to channel your feelings into something positive, rather than leaving you feeling helpless as I initially did.

Step 4 – Do not be put off or distracted by nay-sayers, your own limiting beliefs, or imposter syndrome.

Face any fears that may appear. Seek help and advice if necessary, but it is for you to take control of your situation and make the right decision for you. I was surprised at how many people advised me against taking on the system lest I make things worse for my daughter. For me, it was inconceivable that I do nothing.

Step 5 – Identify the process by which you will achieve your desired outcome.

What do you want out of this? Focus on the possibilities ahead as you learn and grow. Is the goal achievable? Should you proceed? Directing your conscious thoughts towards finding a way through to a satisfactory solution will ensure your personal growth out of the whole process. I sought out relevant experts in the field to find out how my daughter could be taught in a manner that enabled her to learn.

Step 6 – Do what is lawfully required to reach your desired outcome.

Simply doing nothing is not enough. If you know that something has to be done and yet do nothing, your feelings of dissatisfaction will continue. It is the **doing something** that will bring satisfaction. Even making a decision to take the matter no further is still your own firm decision. In my own example, I felt like giving up many times, but I knew that if I did not see it through, I would have never forgiven myself! Therefore, do all that you can to further your own objectives.

Step 7 - Celebrate!

You must always celebrate the fact that you took control of your situation, made a decision on how to deal with it, and were then able to move on. It is very important that the outcome of your decision, be it to change your mind or to change the world, is celebrated.

That brings closure to that aspect of your life, however small or big. It will remain as a pleasant memory of how and why you are now enjoying the position you find yourself in today. Instead of looking back and wondering where it all went wrong and remaining there, you can now use your new-found self knowledge and personal growth to spur you on into a future where you will no longer allow circumstances to dictate your mood or your actions. You will instead take control of your own life, full of unlimited possibilities.

This crucial step brings to mind an old Swahili warrior song which goes something like this: Life has meaning only in the struggle. Triumph or defeat is in the hands of the Gods. So let us celebrate the struggle!

BIO

Chineme has a long career as a lawyer, success coach, and international speaker. She is an award winning author for her book *Special Hidden Talents*, and has multiple Amazon #1 bestsellers.

Her expertise is in all round "Obstacle and Challenge" obliteration - with ease. She does this by dealing effectively with what she calls the mountains and molehills that success seekers encounter in their daily lives, by following her seven step action plan from her first published book, *There is No Time like the Present to Create Your Future*.

She is the founder of the Unstoppable Bizpreneurship program and the Unstoppable Shepreneurs private facebook group, as well as the author of the soon to be published, *Unstoppable Shepreneurs: Become An Emboldened and Empowered Woman, Live An Exceptional Life and Leave Your Legacy*.

Follow her on social media @ChinemeNoke

LinkedIn: www.linkedin.com/in/chinemenoke

TAKE THE BRAKES OFF YOUR DREAMS AND BREAKTHROUGH TO YOUR UNLIMITED POSSIBILITIES

By LaTalya Palmer

When do you pump your brakes? In your vehicle, brakes are the safety mechanisms that keep you from navigating recklessly down your plotted path. However, in your personal life, when you pump the brakes on your dreams, you limit your ability to experience the life you deserve.

You may be pumping the brakes on your dreams out of fear of success, failure, or losing control; and it is leaving you stuck in the safety zone. When you take your foot off the brakes to your dreams, you will travel down a path you never dreamed imaginable. Whether it's past trauma or current adversity that's causing paralysis, from this point on, you get to determine which course you want to take.

I want to share 5 common brakes we put on our dreams and how to breakthrough so you can experience your unlimited potential.

5 Common Brakes are:

1. Doubt
2. Fear

3. Lack of self-belief
4. Pity
5. Confusion

Tips to Break Through to Your Limitless Possibilities!

1. **From Doubt to Dare:** Doubt leads to disregarding your intuition and makes you feel indecisive and uncertain. Ignoring your creative ideas chips away at your ability to act on your dreams. Doubt has put on major brakes for me. For years, I've doubted my gifts and impact. I want to share what's helped me soar.

   For the next 5 days, pay attention to when you doubt yourself. When doubt arises, shift those thoughts and dare to believe in yourself. Dare to trust yourself. Dare to fall in love with your dream and recommit to it in every moment. Imagine feeling trust in your creativity and allowing your ideas to flow. Give yourself permission to override doubt and dare to take bold action in the direction of your dreams.

2. **From Fear to Flame:** Fear doesn't have to control or cripple you. Here is a transformational visualization that's helped me minimize my fears. Imagine flames blazing bright. Now see your fears (one by one) being engulfed by the flames. The flames are burning through the fear, healing the residual pain and trauma. Feel the flame growing and transforming your fear into passion. You feel the flame lighting up your vision, energizing your dreams and you are at peace. Break free from your fears and allow the flame vs. fear to occupy your thoughts.

3. **From Lack of Self-belief to Limitless Confidence:** Imagine a child that you absolutely love standing in front of you. The child shared that she wants to become the world's greatest doctor. She shares her plans to heal children and make their

lives better. All the while she has the most joyous smile on her face. She stops and waits for you to speak. You smile, look the child in the eyes and tell her that you don't believe she can become the world's greatest doctor. There are too many obstacles in her way. You watch her fall apart emotionally but then pull herself together. She rebuts and says, "Yes I can. I know I can. I feel it in my heart. I see it like it's real." And you begin to list every reason becoming the greatest doctor is not possible for her. She still mentions it periodically, only to be met by your lack of belief in her. Soon she stops talking about it and her dream vanishes.

This is what we do to ourselves. We take a stake and drive it through the heart of our dreams. Let's vow in this moment to stand in the face of lack of self-belief and breathe confidence into our lives. Breathe confidence into your abilities, your worth, your dreams, and your purpose. Know without a shadow of a doubt that who you are matters. Know that what you offer matters to the people you are here to serve. Have confidence in your ability to see a project through. Have confidence in your ability to make a powerful impact. Stand tall and know that the energy of your confidence will shine through. Don't give up on you.

4. **From Pity to Power:** How often do you feel shamed, let-down? How many times do you look over your life and recall who did you wrong? It may feel natural to nurture pain but be aware that the longer you dwell on an infraction, the further you spiral downward. You may begin to convince yourself that you are not enough, that something is wrong with you, and that you are not worthy.

It took some time for me to learn that instead of finding comfort in pity, I had to allow myself to grow from the pain. I did this by facing my feelings and learning from my experiences. This is a courageous path that opens you up to your source of power. Through divorce, the loss of my mother, and cancer, I fully realized that there is power in my perseverance. There was power in my ability to get out of the bed when I thought I couldn't. There was power in holding my head up amid the embarrassment of becoming a divorced single mom. Once I released the pity, I got to experience the power granted from your higher power that can't be dimmed by any circumstance.

5. **From Confusion to Clarity:** The state of confusion keeps you stuck and uncertain about where to concentrate your actions and focus your energy. Clarity gives you back your power of intention and focus. It allows your concentrated energy to gain momentum and manifest your intended goal. When you find yourself unclear, I want you to slow down, breathe, check within, and make a decision. Decisiveness is the ultimate cure for confusion.

As we close, please allow this to sink in: "Your dreams uninhibited propel your life forward. Your dreams unhinged require the giant in us to show up and show out. You have what it takes to live a life of unlimited possibilities. All brakes off and all bets on you"!

BIO

LaTalya Palmer, The Dream Igniter, has been in the empowerment industry for 20+ years. She is a Certified Empowerment Trainer and Law of Attraction Coach that helps others turn their adversities into fuel to achieve their dreams. She has gone from generational welfare to earning six figures and has a passion for helping women ignite their personal power and release their victim story.

LaTalya is no stranger to thriving through adversity. In a five-year period, she got divorced, lost her mom to lupus, and was diagnosed with the rare and highly aggressive inflammatory breast cancer. Despite it all, she is here today, thriving, sharing her story, and inspiring others to Ignite and live a full life. During her fight with breast cancer, she self-published her first book *IGNITE! The Single Mother's Guide to Success, Sensuality and Achieving Your Dreams* and continues to nurture and love on her four children.

https://www.instagram.com/coachlatalya

https://www.facebook.com/LifeDesignCoach

https://www.linkedin.com/in/coachlatalya/

FROM WOUNDED WOMAN TO LIVING AN EMPOWERED LIFE

By Dr. Tamiko Lowry Pugh

I remember thinking that I had met the man of my dreams. He was charming, financially stable, had a great smile, dressed nice, and smelled good. Ladies, y'all know we love a good-smelling man. In a nutshell, he was the epitome of "tall, dark, and handsome." In the beginning, he treated me like a queen, always complimenting my looks, my smile, and how smart I was. He loved my outgoing and vivacious personality, even said that he had never met anyone like me.

After dating for a few months, we became inseparable, spending all of our free time together. Though I was enjoying the moment, things were really moving fast. After a few months, we were engaged. In less than a year, we were married.

It wasn't long after we were married that the man of my dreams became my worst nightmare. The compliments he once showered me with turned into insults and criticism. He became very hostile and angry, having random emotional and verbal outbursts. His once loving tone of voice turned harsh and brash. *What had I got myself into?*

Over the next few years, I was beaten emotionally, mentally, verbally, and spiritually, and then eventually physically. Before he had ever laid a hand on me, I was already a broken soul. I remember on several occasions being strangled until I almost passed out, and thinking to myself, "I'm about to die." But the most horrific incident happened the day that I decided to leave. I woke up alone, in a state of confusion and panic, helplessly lying in the middle of the interstate. Just hours before, I had made the decision to finally leave my abuser. As I drove down the interstate, he sat in the passenger seat threatening to kill the both of us if I left. The next thing I knew, he grabbed the steering wheel, forced the car onto the side of the highway, and proceeded to beat and strangle me to the point of unconsciousness. Thankfully, someone saw what happened and called the police. I thought for sure I was going to die on that day. My life flashed before my eyes. I made it out, but not everyone does.

Starting my life all over again was scary. I had hit rock bottom. I was mentally and emotionally broken, and financially broke. I was now a single parent, working a part-time job, barely making enough money to pay my bills and feed my children. There were so many doubts, fears, and uncertainties. Did I make the right decision to leave my husband and our 7-bedroom home? What if I got evicted? Where was our next meal gonna come from?

I cried out to God to give me an answer. Why did I have to go through these painful and hard times? I remember sitting in the church pew asking God, "Why me?" The pastor was preaching a sermon on turning your pain into purpose. "God didn't deliver you from that abusive relationship for nothing," he said. "There was a reason behind it. There is purpose out of that pain." It was one of those moments when you think the pastor is talking directly to you. He was preaching from Romans 8:28(ESV) that says, "And we know that for those who love God all things work together for good, for those who are called according to his purpose." At that moment, I knew my purpose in life. Tears began to flow as I thanked and praised God for uncovering my "why." My pain became my purpose, and my wounds turned into wisdom: the wisdom that I would later share with thousands of women worldwide who were going through what I had survived.

The realization and manifestation of my destiny came when I least expected. I was obedient to God's word and used my story as a tool and resource to help other women. As a result, I began to get requests for paid speaking engagements, community partnerships, and media appearances. Trusting God and living according to Romans 8:28 helped me take my first steps on my path to survivorship, financial independence, and living an empowered life!

I had no idea that something so painful and traumatic would push me into my life's purpose. I had no idea that I'd become a frontline domestic violence advocate, serving as the founder of my own non-profit organization that focuses on domestic violence advocacy, awareness, and prevention. I had no idea that my past adversities would position me to become the CEO of my very own successful coaching company and business academy, which empowers women to use their life experiences and story to create transformational businesses of their own. I had no idea that I would go from being a "wounded woman walking" to *Living The Empowered Life!*

Everything that we experience in life has a reason, a purpose, and a lesson that serves us. Regardless of your situation or what you are going through, it will eventually work together, uncovering God's plan and purpose for your life.

In this season of your life, I encourage you to view every wound or adversity as an educational assignment. Whatever it is that you are experiencing, always ask yourself, "What's the lesson in this?" Whatever that lesson may be, learn from it, and draw purpose from it.

> *"Wisdom is not always measured by what you know but rather how you embrace your wounds of experiences."*

> –Dr. Tamiko

BIO

Dr. Tamiko Lowry Pugh, often referred to as The Empowering Diva, is a voice for women empowerment.

As the Chief Empowerment Officer of Living The Empowered Life LLC, Tamiko leads courses, events, and programs that empower women to uncover their God-given purpose, ignite their confidence, and fearlessly walk in their authentic power.

Dr. Tamiko serves as the host of Living The Empowered Life Podcast. She shares inspirational interviews, tips, tools, and resources that move listeners forward in faith, life, and business. She is also the founder of The Still Standing Alliance, a nonprofit organization that focuses on domestic violence advocacy, awareness, and prevention.

As a survivor of domestic violence, Tamiko is very transparent about her journey of survivorship. This has allowed her to construct a powerful movement dedicated to the empowerment and personal development of women worldwide. She is a compassionate mentor and friend, an enthusiastic leader, and a visionary.

Learn more at www.tamikolowry.com

POSSIBILITIES ARE UNLIMITED WHEN SPEAKING WITH CONFIDENCE & SELF-LOVE

By Saniya I. Reed

When I was in third grade, I was bullied because of the way I dressed. This may have happened to you too. Growing up, I loved to wear dresses and fancy shoes. Wearing dresses made me feel happy and beautiful. My classmates didn't like that I loved to dress fancy.

On Valentine's Day one school year, I was passing out cards to my classmates. I had on my favorite *Hello Kitty* dress with my sparkly pink shoes.One of my classmates asked me, "Why do you always wear dresses?"

I replied, "What do you mean?"

She said, "I don't like you because you like to be fancy and wear fancy clothes."

I was confused. Really. Like, who wouldn't like you because of the way you dress? She continued to be mean and had others agreeing with her. After school was over that day, I went home and cried out to my mother. I was only seven when this happened. As a result of that episode, I shut all the way down until I was ten.

During that time, my father kept asking me, "Are you okay? You do know you can tell me anything."

I kept telling him I was okay even though it wasn't true. I really went through that for three years and never told anyone. After that incident and up through my last couple of years in school, I would see more and more bullying take place amongst my friends.

I want you to think about that little girl hurting and not wanting to tell anyone what happened to her because she was so scared of being judged. I was hurting so bad that I would cry just thinking about it. When my parents would ask why I was crying, I would make up a lie. I would say something like, "My stomach hurts," when I was actually hurting from the pain of being bullied and trying to hold it all in.

If you are a parent, have one-on-one conversations with your kids. Pay close attention to your conversations with them and pay closer attention to what they do. You need to have a close relationship with your kids so they can come to you whenever they need to. Even when they seem to need space, they may actually need to talk. My dad and I had a close relationship, but I was so scared of my parents possibly telling someone about what had happened to me. I thought I would be judged. Deep down, I knew my parents wouldn't, but I was still afraid.

Bullying should not be a normal thing. Even though we can't control what other children do, we can do our part with our children. As a parent, you can talk to your kids about accepting others for who they are. We can work to build our children's confidence so what other people do or say does not change the way they see themselves.

Back to my story...

After spending the evening really thinking about why the girl in class didn't like me, I realized it wasn't me that she didn't like. She didn't like herself. The next day--hurting on the inside with a smile on my face--I returned to class and asked the teacher to allow me to teach a selfie class. I was allowed to teach the class, and when the class was over, the bully realized she was beautiful. It worked!

In my heart, after walking through that tough time in my life, I wanted to do more to help others build confidence. Today, I call the selfie lesson *Capturing Confidence*. I developed this blueprint so that you and everyone in this world can carry confidence with you. The following are the same steps I taught my entire third grade class.

In order to be confident, you have to believe you're a **DIVA**. A diva walks around with poise and with certain thoughts about herself. Here are the steps of a *DIVA.*

Step 1:

D - Don't EVER speak negatively about yourself.

The way we talk to ourselves communicates to the rest of the world. We have to be careful of our thoughts and the words we say because our inner voice will control the confidence that other people see. So, if you want others to love you, it's important for you to love yourself first.

Step 2:

I - IMAGINE - Imagine yourself as the most CONFIDENT person in the room.

You will always be the person you are able to see. Remember to talk and walk with your head held high.

Step 3:

V - Validation - Get used to validating yourself.

Know who you are so you don't seek validation from other people. Their opinion of you is none of your business. Their opinion of you doesn't make you rich.

The last step happens to be my favorite!

Step 4:

A - Awaken - Awaken your inner beauty through your own lens.

It is important to awaken your inner beauty and capture it from the outside. We do this through taking a selfie.

Now let's practice.

Stand up!

Place your hand on your hip!

Hold your head up high!

Straighten up your back to have a powerful pose!

Pull out your camera and capture ALL of your confidence!

You are BEAUTIFUL. You are SMART. You are BRAVE.

Now, BE CONFIDENT.

I share my story and message to teach others how to maintain their own confidence in the face of adversity or unkindness, but I also ask that you help me change the way we build self-confidence for kids.

Having confidence helps you to achieve your goals in life. Without confidence we won't have courage to do the things that make us "go bigger" in life.

Once a person captures their confidence and learns to carry it with them every day, the possibilities in life will be UNLIMITED!

I have started a coaching program for young girls, ages 7-11, called *Be the Light*. I have also designed an inspirational product line called

Digital Diva that carries apparel and accessories to help build confidence in young girls.

You can connect with me on all social media platforms at @IAmSaniyaReed. To find out more information about products and services, go to www.www.saniyaireed.com

BIO

Saniya I. Reed is a 3x #1 best-selling author and certified speaker who has a desire to change the world.

Since childhood, Saniya has been known to be an independent and observant problem solver. She has a passion for fashion and embraced style at an early age. This led her to designing her inspirational product line, *Digital Diva,* that inspires young girls to capture their confidence through the lens of their own camera.

Saniya is studying to become a certified Wisdom & Confidence Coach to launch her new program, *Be the Light,* for young girls ages 7-11. Her goal is to travel the world, share her message,and help others spread confidence.

Saniya's been able to meet and deliver her work to Hollywood star, Tiffany Haddish, and has been featured on ABC, CNN, CBS and BlackNews.com Saniya's signature messages address building confidence, finding self-love and eradicating peer-to-peer bullying.

Website: www.saniyaireed.com

Instagram: @IAmSaniyaReed

DEFINING YOUR OWN WORTH

By Effie Robertson

"But as for you, ye thought evil against me;
but God meant it unto good, to bring to pass, as it is this day,
to save much people alive."

– Genesis 50:20 (KJV)

"Please help me! Please help me!"

I cried for aid as my nude body dangled outside the window and he grabbed my legs and pulled me back into the room. The cold metal sill began to slice my abdomen as he pulled me back through the window. I could see the neighbors sitting on the porch, sipping their beers and puzzlingly staring up at me through the window. My skull smacked onto the hardwood floor, then he tossed my body across the room. As I hammered into the wall closest to the bed, my body came to a rest. Frightened, I gazed up at his face as I attempted to catch my breath. He had caught me, and now I was in serious trouble. I was going to pay the price for my failed escape attempt.

It had already been at least twenty-four hours since he'd forced me into the padlocked bedroom. Because two teenagers resided in the apartment with their mother, the place was normally buzzing with people in and out at all hours of the day. Later, I discovered that the family had spent the weekend at a friend's house, making it the ideal opportunity for him to torture me for four days and three nights.

I didn't expect the neighbors to help me. The abuse had been going on for three years, and by this time, friends, family and the neighborhood was immune to our wrath. Over time, our conflicts became increasingly violent and terrifying. So, for the most part, this stage of escalation was unsurprising. He meticulously planned to isolate me on this specific weekend and inflict pain on me in unimaginable ways. Punishment for my attempt to flee through the window was him grabbing my neck and strangling me until I passed out. I woke up to him yelling and stomping my body with his size thirteen bare feet. He repeated these strangulations until he completely tired himself into exhaustion. I was collapsed in the hall closet beneath a pile of clothes when I finally awoke from the last strangulation. To this day, I'm convinced he thought I was dead and was trying to figure out how to dispose of my remains.

Those four days and three nights with him were pure agony. He would rape me for hours with relentless brutality and malice until he would fall asleep on top of me. When the rape wasn't enough to satiate his rage, I was beaten with a crowbar. My body was black and blue. There were multiple broken bones in my arms and fingers. Every time I stood to extend my legs, blood dripped from my shredded flesh.

My escape occurred when his sister returned home, and her teenagers forced the door off the hinges. My final escape was swift. If I had been challenged, I believe I could have outrun Jackie Joyner-Kersee at that moment. I was running for my life!

New Beginnings

I ran four states away. Living in the same city was too terrifying for me, especially because the courts' only sanction against him was a fine of a few hundred dollars. Years of abuse left me with feelings of unworthiness, confusion, and self-doubt. I was a complete mess. I spent the majority of the next few years broke and homeless. Every day, I cursed God for abandoning me. I cursed him for my internal struggle.

One day, I resolved to put an end to it all. I began to sob uncontrollably after swallowing half a bottle of prescription medications, imploring God, *"Why? Why me?"* Immediately, I could feel an energy wrapping itself around my body and holding me so tightly that I almost felt suffocated. As the tears streamed down my face, my soul began to ache. I was a chaos of emotions. I was terrified, confused, and angry, but I gained an overwhelming desire to try and be better. I wanted to do and be better. I wanted to be something other than a victim, someone other than my circumstances. I wanted to live!

After that night, I became intentional about life. I decided to make a conscious effort in my life. I'd pray to God and beg for guidance and clarity. As I reflected on my life, I realized that my self-worth had been tainted prior to that relationship due to the years of sexual trauma I endured. I'd never felt worthy, and it showed in the four years I spent being abused by a man I thought I loved. One step at a time, it was time to break those chains of defeat. My daily affirmation was short and simple: My past, present, nor any future circumstances will ever define me again.

This affirmation donned my mirror and I repeated it daily. I grew stronger and put forth more effort. My life's vision expanded. My self-assurance rose, and I began to believe that I was deserving of everything that manifested in my life.

In My Pursuit of Possibilities

"When your life is on course with its purpose,
you are the most powerful."

– Oprah Winfrey

God had something else in mind for me. After graduating from nursing school, I quickly advanced up the corporate ladder. Within two years of graduating, I was working for a Fortune 500 firm and managing three hundred employees. Won't God turn a mess into a masterpiece? I now believed I was deserving. I had a place in the world to fill, and the possibilities I could create were endless. I decided to pursue entrepreneurship, and my first company made over six figures in its first year. Although the company dissolved when the marriage to my first husband ended, it did not destroy my ambitions to pursue other business opportunities with my current husband.

Today, as I venture on a new path for our company and take larger risks, I am thrilled to share that I'm finally at peace in my heart, mind and soul. My past once gripped me so tightly that I was on the verge of laying down my life like a sacrificial lamb. A budding rose has replaced the charcoal-lined boundaries of my shame. Not as a consequence of my abuse, but as a result of it, I am now complete. Every layer of agony and every shattered piece has been reborn as a new life...a new beginning. I've reclaimed control of my life and created one that truly belongs to me.

I strongly advise you to never give up on yourself. 'Doubt' and 'impossible' should be banished from your vocabulary.

Begin to show up for yourself every day with an attitude that is based on belief and possibility. Stop making excuses and start pursuing your goals with persistent determination. Begin where you are and work your way up from there, while relying on God's promise. The key to living in your phenomenal purpose and creating unlimited possibilities is simply believing that all things are possible.

BIO

Effie Robertson is a best-selling author, Master Resilience Coach, inspirational speaker, and CEO of SimplyMonei' and FieldingDreams365 LLC. She holds an MBA from the University of Management and Technology. She sits on the board for the nonprofit organization, Sanctuary Foundation for Veterans. Effie is a wife and devoted mother of three children. She is passionate about uplifting and empowering people to live the legacy they desire by realizing their own potential, purpose, and destiny.

Following her chapter, "Defining Your Own Worth," in this anthology project, Effie plans to release an autobiography, in which she demonstrates the ability to bounce back from physical and sexual abuse. Her story will show courage and instill hope, while inspiring readers to change from victim to conqueror. Effie's personal life story is mesmerizing, captivating, and transformational.

You can connect with Effie at:

Email: FieldingDreams365@gmail.com

Websites: www.effierobertson.com

www.simplymonei.com

JUST KEEP SHOWING UP

By Dr. Sanja Rickette Stinson

As a child, my vision was to attend college, earn the highest education possible, and become an entrepreneur, following my parents' footsteps. Despite graduating from high school with a deficiency in reading reflecting in my grades and continued struggles with a speech impediment, discouragement from others around me, including educators, and experiencing ongoing racial disparities as a woman of color, I achieved the highest level of education, earning a doctorate. In addition, during my adult years, I became an entrepreneur, even though several of my first attempts failed. I continued to show up. I share this not to be boastful, but to show you the power that unfolds when you *keep showing up.*

Currently, I serve as the founding CEO of a nonprofit organization in the Midwest. It was a startup that is now celebrating thirty-two years in operation. To view the organization now, many would see it as successful, as it has existed beyond the first five, ten, or even fifteen years startup businesses are expected to last. However, there were many times that the organization experienced severe struggles that should have shut it down. But this never negated my strong faith, due to my upbringing as a Christian. Having faith is great, for I am so aware it is "the substance of things hoped for, the evidence of things not seen" (Hebrews 11:1).

I also must have contributed to the organization's success because despite the many struggles to pay staff, I and others kept showing up. We showed up because, first, we were committed to the organization's mission to serve the homeless, and second, because we believed that things would get better soon. So, despite no pay for quite a while, we decided to *keep showing up*. As the organization grew, our ability to secure funding improved as funders began to notice our outstanding work. Things eventually improved, and the organization secured a more significant grant to provide permanent supported housing for homeless individuals and raise additional unrestricted funding to support some much-needed administrative staff.

Then, some years later, an audit threatened to derail our success and possibly shut the organization down. "But God" is all I will say here! The nonprofit began to experience significant cash flow struggles, resulting in not meeting payroll and other accountant payable obligations. Payrolls were delayed, late, and sometimes deferred. Some of the staff chose to leave, and I clearly understood. Not only did they need to survive, but they needed to be able to provide for their families. The majority of staff chose to stay and wait out the temporary setback. When I asked why they didn't take the option of leaving and collecting unemployment, many said, "We are committed to the vision and mission and how you *keep showing up*." The audit lasted longer than expected and shut down a huge portion of our funding. The organization was aware and committed to changing things and putting approved corrective action plans in place. Also, we hired an additional consultant with the expertise needed to begin the corrective action which was needed to restore our funding. It was no secret that the auditor was often unfair and cantankerous, no matter how hard the organization worked on our action plan. Those who supervised the auditor deemed the organization's treatment unfair. However, no matter the struggles, the remaining staff and I *just kept showing up*. It is challenging to fully tell the story in one chapter.

As we celebrate thirty-two years as a nonprofit organization, we are the only daytime supportive center providing services to homeless individuals in our area. Those who remained said they had experienced worth and believed we could get through the rough patch and win. So, each day, the staff and I showed up with one purpose: to serve individuals experiencing homelessness. Faith was a key factor. However, the ability to *keep showing up* was also a significant contributing factor. Despite the unlimited possibilities when you *just keep showing up*, there is no doubt that showing up is hard, especially when there are delayed results and rewards. But the real journey is in the showing up. It can lead to limitless possibilities and lots of new opportunities.

The power of showing up builds character, reveals courage, opens up new connections, and promotes real collaboration. Showing up is a journey that will stretch you. The value of showing up demonstrates that you are a champion and that you belong there, whether others believe it or show up in support of you or not. Showing up reveals that you have decided to walk in your purpose. Today, I encourage you, if you haven't been showing up, start today. There will be a time when the situation appears hopeless; show up anyway. Showing up can change the trajectory of any situation. So, there is power when you can *just keep showing up*, resulting in you experiencing the unlimited possibilities for the life you prefer to live.

Here is the call to start showing up:

1) Don't allow fear to prevent you from showing up; show up even if you're scared.
2) Your vision will take a little while; show up and await its arrival.
3) There is a winner in you; start showing up with a winning posture.
4) Know that there will be a time when you don't feel like showing up; get up and show up despite your feelings.
5) The battle is won when you *just keep showing up.*

Are you ready to show up? It will be worth it to you to *just keep showing up.*

BIO

At the heart of philanthropy lies resolute leadership encompassed vessels fastened to an unyielding mandate to serve others. Owning this distinction in prolific measure is the compassionate professional, Dr. Sanja Rickette Stinson. Growing up with a respect for business and humanity, affluent in the sentimental language of people, she holds her roots of generational legacy, entrepreneurship and ministry from her entrepreneurial parents, Gus & Mary Rickette, the proud founders of Uncle Remus Saucy Chicken in Chicago. Her parents' example fostered a strong advocacy for the merger of marketplace and ministry she reveres as priceless. She is an author, cleric, serial entrepreneur and CEO of Matthew House, a daytime center serving homeless men, women, children, and families for over 30 years. Dr. Stinson earned her Bachelor's degree from DePaul University, a Master of Divinity from McCormick Theological Seminary, a Master of Education from Concordia University,and a Doctorate of Ministry from Northern Theological Seminary. www.drsanja.com

THE EXCEPTIONAL WOMAN

By Michelle S. Thomas

Throughout my journeys, I've been blessed to have met some amazing women from all walks of life. These are women I looked up to not just for their positions in power or their financial statuses, but because they exhibited an unshakable inner sense of self. Some of these impactful women have very little social media presence, and they don't run Fortune 500 companies or have loads of money. They are everyday women doing great things for their families, communities, and strangers because they all accepted their divinely appointed assignments. They are exceptional women.

The exceptional woman is a woman who knows there is someone out there who needs her to show up with clarity and consistency. She's a woman who is driven by her ethics, integrity, and the unexplained joy she feels when she sees someone else win. God blessed me to be surrounded by exceptional women, which helped shape me into the exceptional woman I strive daily to be. Some of these women may not be an active part of my life anymore, as some have passed and others were around for only a season. Whether they knew it or not, they left a lasting impact on my life. I still pay homage to their essence.

I grew up in a family full of very strong women like my aunts Janice, Inez, Evelyn, and Essie. Each one of them corrected me when I was wrong, celebrated me for my wins, and spoke wisdom into my life. They carried me through my most vulnerable times while constantly reminding me that "this too shall pass." When I was younger, I didn't grasp the value of each of the seeds they selflessly planted in me. However, when God knew it was time for each seed to be harvested, I reaped an enriched toolbox of principles that I needed to find success. Over the years, countless women have effortlessly taught, molded, and uplifted me by constantly giving of themselves and patiently showing me the way to overcome adversities, pain, rejection and loss. More than anything, though, they taught me how to stop moving so fast to celebrate the good times. Women like Natalie Williams and Dr. Cheryl Wood made sure I understood the importance of preparation, evaluation and valuation of every business move I made. Sharon Bedford gave me permission to "be ME." And of course, my mother, Rosa Spears, showed me how to present grace and elegance. This message is not about me traveling down memory lane. Instead, it's my way of honoring the ancestral ways of the exceptional women in my life and paying it forward.

Being an exceptional woman doesn't mean life won't impact you negatively or tragically. Being an exceptional woman means you will embrace and elevate graciously throughout anything placed in your path. You know your story, but you don't necessarily have to "look like" your story. You have a presence about you that forces people to gravitate towards your light, even when you don't feel like you're at the top of your game. As you read this today, affirm yourself that you ARE an exceptional woman, and despite any circumstances that may come your way, you WILL succeed! This prestigious honor should not be taken lightly nor practiced sparingly. You must commit to this lifestyle consciously and consistently.

Fully investing in your exceptional life requires a physical, mental, and emotional commitment. Studies have shown that your physical well-being can be altered by your emotional state. Stress, negative feelings, and depression can slow the natural production of the hormones that control your ability to feel happy. It sounds rudimentary, but improve your physical self and your mental health will follow. Modern luxuries and technology have caused us to spend most of our days sitting. Running errands or working is not enough to stimulate the dopamine and serotonin that our minds need to feel positive. A regiment of at least 30 minutes of daily exercise or physical activity can improve your mental well-being tremendously. Remember, all of the impactful women I mentioned before? Well, the one thing they had in common was their active lifestyles. Their support was not just verbal. They were physically present. Whoever or whatever needed their attention, they gave their all. Even if they were tired, they never allowed that to hinder their purpose.

Your mental state is based on your ability to process the information being delivered to you. If you find yourself reacting dramatically to every situation, you must strengthen your mental state. The exceptional woman manages situations, instead of allowing them to manage her. Plans not working out as you expected? Then gracefully shift. Always prepare for the "what ifs" that can happen at the most inopportune times.

And lastly, protect your emotions. Be intentional with your choices, professional and personal. You must learn to value your time and space. Anything or anyone that does not positively uplift your life, limit the amount of their presence within your precious space. Even the strongest of us cannot deflect constant negative energies. Without realizing it, if you're too often present with negativity, you may find yourself emulating adverse behaviors that can alter your own energy. Reflection is good. However, remaining focused on the past can become a form of self-sabotaging. Have you ever thought yourself into depression? You wake up feeling good and hopeful. Then, throughout the day, thoughts of what did not happen, what didn't go right, or what could have been quickly sink you into the blues. Learn to interrupt that impulse and redirect your thoughts into more positive reflections.

As the exceptional woman you are, focus on the impact you present to those around you. Give more than you take, and you will find your life being continuously enriched with more than you could ever dream. Your legacy will far outlive your time on this earth. Plant those seeds and watch how another exceptional woman pays homage to you, just as I have done to the exceptional women in my life.

BIO

Michelle S. Thomas, Your Relationship Surgeon, is a 5X International Best-Selling Author, Certified Life/Relationship/Business Coach, and multiple business owner. She serves individuals and businesses by precisely pinpointing what is "infecting" their ability to achieve PEACE, PROSPERITY and PROFITABILITY while placing them on a permanent path to success. Michelle uplifts women globally through her trademarked summit **"The EXCEPTIONAL Woman Tour"**, her learning platforms, philanthropic endeavors, and nonprofit organizations. Connect with Your Relationship Surgeon today by visiting www.michellesthomas.com. For more information on The EXCEPTIONAL Woman Tour visit: www.exceptionalwomantour.com. Follow Michelle on FB/IG @ yourrelationshipsurgeon.

SURVIVING SUICIDAL IDEATION

By Willie Mae Starr-White

According to the CDC, suicide is the 10th leading cause of death in the US for all ages. Suicide takes the lives of 48,500 people every year in the US.

If you're feeling suicidal, you're not alone. I lived through suicidal thoughts of feeling severely unworthy, unimportant, and unloved.

I'm alive to tell this story of how I overcame a fate I thought I surely deserved. After I had my son, I was diagnosed with lupus and rheumatoid arthritis. Then, I was later diagnosed with depression. I had to take so many pills. I remember feeling like no one cared about me. I was so tired of defending myself. I was a single parent and struggled daily. No one believed me when I tried to explain how I felt. I stuttered severely, and no one had the patience to listen to me. I had low self-esteem and a great sense of worthlessness.

It was Saturday, September 17, 2002. I remember sending my son to school, writing him a farewell note, apologizing for what I was about to do and telling him I loved him so much. At that point, I recall taking 25-30 Plaquenil tablets. I started having abdominal cramps and hoped what I'd taken was adequate to end my life. As I began to fade and fatigue took over, I thought of my son. What was I doing to my child? I realized that although I felt I was alone and had no support, if I died, my son would be alone and feel the same way.

I remember calling 911 and telling them I had made a grave mistake and didn't want to die. I don't know when the paramedics arrived. I recall waking up in the ER at UPMC Braddock. I didn't expect to be alive. Thank you, Jesus! I felt guilty, ashamed, and honestly, embarrassed because of my suicide attempt. All I could do was cry and ask God for forgiveness. I had never had suicidal thoughts before. Why did I do that?

The doctor introduced himself and asked if I had ever had suicidal thoughts before. I told him I never had.

He explained that some antidepressants could cause suicidal thinking and sometimes worsen depression. It was discovered that I had bipolar depression disorder rather than depression. I was misdiagnosed and was taking the wrong medication. I learned that it's critical to get a second opinion before committing to taking antidepressants for the rest of your life.

So, what is bipolar depression disorder? Bipolar depression disorder is a condition that creates severe mood swings. You can feel energetic, euphoric, or agitated one moment, and feel down and completely hopeless the next moment. The "lows" you may feel...those moments of hopelessness...these are the possible symptoms of the depressive moments associated with bipolar depression disorder. **If any of this sounds familiar or like something you've experienced, it is imperative to explain all your symptoms to your doctor, whether you think they are relevant or not. It's crucial to educate oneself and understand depression and what's normal and abnormal.**

Mental health is vital. It encompasses our psychological, emotional, and overall well-being. It affects how we socialize, feel, and think. It also helps us handle stress and make rational decisions. Mental health is essential at every stage of life, from childhood to adolescence and on through adulthood. At every stage, mental illness is prevalent and treatable, but some people won't get assistance with mental illness due to its stigma. Many people view mental illness as dangerous, weak, unstable, or unreliable. This stereotype can make it more challenging for them to get help. The Covid pandemic alone has had a profound impact on the mental health of people of all ages. Please seek the help you need. Stop trying to remedy yourself.

What are some of the causes of suicide? A combination of situations can lead someone to entertain thoughts of suicide. Suicidal ideation may be caused by the following:

- previous suicide attempts
- mental illness, such as depression
- social isolation due to confinement
- financial problems
- bullying problems
- impulsive or aggressive tendencies
- job problems or loss
- legal problems
- serious illness
- social media exposure
- substance use disorder
- relationship problems
- sexual violence
- misdiagnosed illnesses

I was only 31 years old and almost took my own life because of an overwhelming sense of feeling unworthy, unimportant, and unloved. Instead of strengthening my faith, I allowed myself to be filled with fear, insecurity, doubt and pity, and I almost robbed myself of the glorious victories God intended for me to have. I almost lost the most precious gift of my life--my son. As I'm writing this chapter, my son is 25 years old. He graduated from California University with a bachelor's degree in computer science. I'm so proud of him!

It's only because of God's mercy that I'm alive. I still ask for forgiveness every day. I continue to ask God to help me to forgive myself. Lord Jesus, thank you.

God loves you! God loves me!

I have learned that life is worth every molecule of oxygen we breathe day to day. Each day, good or bad, is a gift. I would have lost it all--my son, my husband, my brother, my family, my friends, my career, and my life. Suicide is not the answer to any problem or situation you find yourself in. If you are experiencing suicidal ideation, please get help immediately. Don't suffer alone because you're not alone. There are so many programs and resources out there. It doesn't matter what you have gone through.

Below are a few suggestions if you're feeling suicidal:

1. Call 911 or the National Suicide Prevention Line at 1-800-273-8255 to get help immediately.
2. Text HOME to 741741 to reach someone who will help you.
3. Strengthen your faith. Call your pastor or prayer partner.
4. Call a close family member or friend and talk to them.
5. Go to your church or the nearest church and ask for help.
6. Call your PCP or doctor. Let them know the thoughts you're having.
7. Get a referral from your PCP to see a psychotherapist/psychiatrist.
8. Visit one of the websites below.

For more information on suicide, visit

- https://suicidepreventionlifeline.org/
- https://suicidepreventionlifeline.org/talk-to-someone-now/
- https://www.dbsalliance.org/

BIO

Entrepreneur\Speaker\Mentor\Author

As a suicide survivor, Willie Mae Starr-White, known as the "Smiling Lady" promises to show that life is always the answer. Her life has taught her strength, faith, resilience, and bravery.

Willie Mae has worked in business administration, facilities management and the records management industry for 25 years. She has learned to develop optimal organizational structures, perform strategic planning, and financial management.

She served in the United States Army for 6 years as a Specialist in the 23rd Postal Unit in Pittsburgh PA.

Willie Mae has been an active member of Toastmasters International for 14 years. She is the 2020-2021 president of BNY Mellon Toastmasters Club. She is enthusiastically working through her Motivational Strategies and Lead Development Pathway Programs.

Willie Mae pulls her strength from her loving husband, intelligent and handsome son, and empowering and protective brother. Her inspiration for writing comes from her nieces, nephews, and family.

OVERCOMING MY BIGGEST OBSTACLE: ME

By Jayana Wood

If someone had told me that I, a young, black, introverted female would be a three-time author, a bestselling novelist, the self-taught body artist of her own henna business, and the founder of an ever-growing streetwear clothing brand, all at the tender age of 17, I likely would have called you crazy and proceeded to laugh until my stomach ached. But, as a young, black, self-employed teenpreneur who is currently living this unexpected reality, the plausibility that the possibilities available in an individual's life are solely defined by the chances they choose to take and the dreams they decide to chase, no longer seems as far-fetched as it used to. Despite how attractive my story might currently appear, it didn't at all start out this way. Even though it may seem as if this thriving black girl has it all put together, my final chapter is far from over. There have been many ups and many downs, plenty of occasions where my doubts overtook my convictions, various moments where I wanted to quit altogether, and overcoming myself as my own biggest obstacle has been a pivotal turning point in my ongoing journey of creating legacy and obtaining success.

When I was growing up, I had always known that I was different from everybody else. Not in a cocky sense where I saw myself as higher above those around me, but in the solemn sense that I never truly felt I had somewhere I belonged. In a room full of lively people, I still managed to feel unbearably lonely. In the midst of indecorous jokes and talks of schoolbound crushes amongst friends, I wasn't able to fully share the conversation—my interests being significantly divergent from theirs. I never really fit in anywhere or with one particular group of people, and it took me a long time to wholeheartedly accept this and genuinely be okay with it. Being different from the perceived normal isn't in any way a bad thing. Rather, it's a beautiful thing that shows you have an abundance of courage--higher than most--to be willing to step outside of your comfort zone and be who *you* want to be without question or regret.

I wasn't always this comfortable with myself—who I was and who I wanted to become. I wasn't always outspoken, I wasn't always confident in my abilities as a business owner, and I certainly didn't always think I had the power to change the world and impact the lives of other young, black business owners like myself. In fact, despite how much I have accomplished for my age, I *still* have days where I revert back to my old bad habits and begin to cross-examine whether or not what I have to say and what I want to do even matters. And despite having started my entrepreneurial journey at the young age of nine, where one would assume I had to have been extremely self-assured to take such a huge leap of faith, it wasn't until now, only two months away from turning 18, and nine long years later, that I am able to confidently say that I know who I am, I know who I want to be, and I am not afraid to own it as fearlessly and as authentically as I can.

Overcoming yourself is, what I believe, to be one of the biggest challenges any person and business owner alike will face when trying to accomplish their goals and achieve their dreams. I used to think it was just a popular mantra anytime I heard someone say, "You can do anything you put your mind to!" But, as a shy, independent, and studious teenager who never thought she would be able to write her first book, start her own henna business, or create her own clothing brand until she took the chance and went for it, I can solidly affirm that this saying is so much more than an overused jumble of words. Nevertheless, as wonderful as it is to be able to confidently present yourself and everything you know you have to offer the world, if any of you reading this chapter today is like me when I first started out—afraid, unsure, and standing in your own way—I want you to know that you are not alone in this journey. I want to help push you out of your shell so you can begin to share your gifts with the rest of the world. So, here are seven key tips that helped me in overcoming myself and allowed me to take the first steps into creating an unforgettable legacy.

Tip #1: Be Patient with Yourself

Everything in life takes time. Nothing worth doing or gaining is ever going to happen overnight. So, be patient with yourself and your journey as you continue to learn and grow along the way.

Tip #2: Find What You Love and Pursue It

If you don't genuinely love what you do, you will not stick with it. So, find what truly moves you and go after it with everything you got. Eat, sleep, and breathe that thing 24/7, and let nothing and no one take that passion away from you.

Tip #3: Get Out of Your Own Head

Your self limitations and how you talk to yourself are extremely critical to your success. Stop hindering your own abilities before you even get the chance to show what you can do. If you think you can't, you won't. But, if you think you can, you will.

Tip #4: Surround Yourself with Like-Minded People

The energy in your space tends to determine how you move and how you feel. So, surround yourself with things, environments, and people who help you and make you feel good, not hurt you and bring you down. Having a strong support system is always beneficial in the long run.

Tip #5: Stay Motivated and Keep Pushing

Motivation and dedication will not always come easy. It is something you have to continuously work at on a daily basis. So, don't give up, even when it gets tough. Keep moving forward. Set new goals for yourself that will force you to keep that drive going strong.

Tip #6: Maintain Balance Between Work and Pleasure

There is always a time and a place for work, and there is always a time and a place for relaxation. It's important to have an even balance of both. When you're feeling stuck or frustrated, don't overwork yourself. It's *okay* to take a break. But, don't stay stagnant for too long. You don't want to start slacking off and lose sight of your end goals and aspirations either.

Tip #7: Be Open to Learning New Things

it's okay to not have all of the answers. It's okay to admit that you don't know everything. Don't ever be ashamed of being open to accepting new advice, especially from those who have more experience than you do. Learning new information will only help you grow and become better in the future. If you aren't learning, you aren't growing, and if you aren't growing, neither is your knowledge or your expertise.

Remember, you got this! The world is your oyster and life is only as big or as small as you choose to make it. Don't let yourself and your own personal doubts fight harder than your desire to impact the world. Someone out there is waiting on *YOU!* So, don't be afraid to get out of your comfort zone. Take the stage front and center and let your light shine bright.

BIO:

Jayana Wood is a creative and artistic 17-year-old writer pursuing a goal of launching her own successful fiction series that will reach readers globally. She is currently a senior in the STEM Program at Oxon Hill High School in Maryland. Jayana is an avid reader, a contributing writer for the school newspaper, and a member of the Drama Club. In her leisure time, she applies her creative prowess to providing henna body art for individuals, parties, and special occasions, and creating custom designs for her clothing brand, *Self Flex*.

Jayana wrote her first book, *Opening My Imagination*, at age 9, and her second book, *The Little Book of Youth Tips*, at age 11. She enjoys inspiring other youth to dream big, pursue their goals, and become leaders who inspire others.

Jayana has been featured in The Baltimore Times, The Washington Informer, Fox 45 News, "Let's Talk Live" News Channel 8, Prince George's County Television, and numerous radio shows. She is the recipient of the 2019 Teen Speaker of the Year Award, the 2016 Youthpreneur of the Year Award, and the 2014 Youthpreneur STAR Award.

Jayana is the proud big sister to two younger brothers—James and Jalen.

Made in USA - Kendallville, IN
67700_9781792382611
01.21.2022 1408